THE APPALACHIAN TRAIL FOOD PLANNER

Interior design by Kathleen Mallow-Sager

© 2001, 2009 Lou Adsmond
Published by the Appalachian Trail Conservancy
799 Washington Street
Harpers Ferry, West Virginia 25425
<www.appalachiantrail.org>

ISBN 978-1-889386-61-4

Second Edition

Printed in the United States of America

The mileage chart in the appendix, from the *Appalachian Trail Thru-Hike Planner,* is
reprinted with permission; copyright 2009 Appalachian Trail Conservancy

THE APPALACHIAN TRAIL

FOOD
PLANNER

Recipes and Menus for a 2,000-Mile Hike

By Lou Adsmond

APPALACHIAN TRAIL
CONSERVANCY ®

Harpers Ferry

Table of Contents

Introduction

When my husband, Alan, and son, Dan, planned a then-2,160-mile "thru-hike" of the Appalachian Trail, I volunteered to prepare and send "food drops" along the way.

A food drop, if you haven't heard the term, gets its name from the old practice of dropping off (sometimes literally, by parachute from an airplane) a package of supplies to backcountry expeditions. On the Appalachian Trail, of course, this isn't necessary, because the Trail never runs very far from such outposts of civilization as post offices, hiking stores, and hostels. Instead of a parachute, the method of delivery is usually the U.S. Postal Service or United Parcel Service (UPS).

Such "mail drops" have become a traditional way that A.T thru-hikers supply themselves along the way. Even today, when a hiker can supplement mail drops with fresh food from the supermarkets in many "Trail towns" and near road crossings, it requires a lot of planning.

For my husband and son, this meant a total of twenty-one packages. They took the first one with them. The rest I shipped out to them over the course of six months. We learned a lot of lessons in the process, and this book is designed to help you learn both from our mistakes and our successes.

In the years since my two thru-hikers completed their journey, we have compared notes with others who have shared their experience with the Appalachian Trail Conservancy. The result is this book, which is both an *idea book*, in which you can see how we planned for our thru-hike and learn from our example, and a *cook book*, with recipes and specific suggestions that you can follow or adapt as needed.

Everyone's hike is different, so don't be surprised when your plans change midway through your thru-hike. You may not even be planning a thru-hike, but rather an extended "section-hike" of a week or more. In either case, you'll find that early preparation makes for a more successful hike. I hope you will find this planner useful.

1 What They Carried

We began planning and researching logistics a full six months before the hike began. The first step was deciding on criteria for the meals on the Trail. These are some that we set for ourselves, and some of the issues we considered:

- *We should never carry more than a six-day supply of food at any one time.*
- *Food weight, per person, should never exceed two pounds per day. (For a full, six-day supply, that would mean a total of twelve additional pounds per person.)*
- *Dinners should require not more than twenty minutes of cooking time; less, if possible.*

- *We should try for as much variety as possible for dinner menus. (Originally, we planned fifteen different dinners. It became more.)*
- *Dinners should have meat, poultry, or fish protein or (if vegetarian) an equivalent complete protein.*

Food Weight

Weight is crucial when planning what food to carry. Long-distance backpackers strive to keep pack weights below fifty pounds, *including* food and water, and many try for a pack that weighs no more than thirty-five or forty pounds. Every ounce a backpacker carries should be worth its weight in "Gorp."

Food Quantities

Our schedule sometimes said "Food for six days" or "Food for three days." In practice, three to four days of food is more usual on the A.T., where hikers rarely face a full six days of wilderness hiking unless they choose to. You will most likely find long hikes between resupply stops only at the southern and northern ends of the Trail, where stores are fewer and farther between. For the thousand-odd miles between central Virginia and New Hampshire, though, you're never more than two or three days from a convenient resupply point, if you wish to keep your pack weight down. Carry more only if you can manage the extra weight and don't want frequent town stops.

The recipes used in this book are for two people, although, in most cases, they can be adapted for one person. Occasionally, a recipe reads for three people. Hikers eat a lot, particularly after the first few weeks on the Trail, so the portions here are large. When you first begin your hike, your appetite may be somewhat smaller than it will be later on, so pick dinner recipes that use two cups of water for cooking rather than one that requires three-and-a-half or four cups.

Frequent nibbling on a trail mix that contains nuts, dried fruits, chocolate, or carob bits will spread your intake of proteins and fats throughout the day, providing long-term energy benefits; the carbohydrates provide quick energy.

Many hikers plan to carry an extra day's supply of food, in case they get held up by bad weather or hurt themselves and can't hike as fast as usual.

In cases when a six-day supply would not carry them to the next convenient post office or hostel, our hikers supplemented their rations by purchasing extra items from a supermarket or general store. With those cases, I included in the mail-drop package a list of food supplies they might purchase until the next package arrived, so they could shop according to a recipe rather than shopping according to whim and the dictates of an empty stomach. Sometimes, they would eat at restaurants in between mail drops, which also extended the time a food package would last.

"Bounce Boxes"

Thru-hikers sometimes send themselves mail drops, too. For instance, after buying large quantities of certain supplies in town to get a cheaper price, they'll sometimes divide the supplies up into halves or thirds and send the extra ahead for a future mail drop. Some hikers use a "bounce box"—a package with nonperishable food and other supplies that they forward ahead to themselves from post office to post office as they walk, rather than carrying the extra weight. Our hikers didn't use this system, but others have done so successfully.

Food Variety

For variety, we planned fifteen basic dinner menus. Our plans eventually expanded to include more. Some of the food we bought prepackaged or in a form (dehydrated or freeze-dried) that could be stored without spoiling. Some we bought ahead of time and dried ourselves, using our ovens and food dehydrators. Some, Alan and Dan bought along the way.

Water

All water along the Appalachian Trail should be treated to remove common microorganisms such as *giardia lamblia*. Common ways of treating water include removing the microbes using a water filter or water purifier, killing them by adding chemicals such as iodine, or boiling. If you're preparing a dinner that requires boiling water anyway, you can sometimes kill two bugs with one stone, so to speak. The water filter used by our hikers was the General Ecology-First Need pump. They were grateful for their filter when several fellow hikers suffering from *giardiasis* found it necessary to leave the Trail

Our hikers found that a three-gallon water bag was important because it was often a steep hike down the side of the mountain to the nearest spring. (A smaller bag would be sufficient for a solo hiker.) Without the water bag, one would have to make several trips to get enough for meal

Although water is plentiful along the Trail during much of the year, in midsummer and early fall, lower-elevation springs sometimes run dry.

preparation, clean-up, and the next day's hike. During the day, most hikers carry liter-size water bottles, or modern "hydration packs," that they drink from as they hike, refilling them when they pass streams and springs. But, trail food usually requires a lot of water for cooking—water you don't want to carry during the day because it's too heavy. A water carrier is worth its weight.

Hikers need to drink a minimum of three to four quarts of water per day when backpacking during the summer, when the greatest amounts are lost in perspiration. In winter, dehydration is easier to miss, but your body needs to be well-hydrated in order to stay warm. Force yourself to drink a lot, even when you don't feel like you're sweating.

Nutrition

Since this was a six-month continuous hike and not just a two-week expedition, nutritional factors were as important as warm clothes and good gear. While researching materials already written on backpacking foods, we found a number of excellent books on the subject, which we have listed at the end of this writing. From these books, we gleaned many helpful tips, recipes, and food for thought.

The nutrition sections of those books were what we took most seriously. As my son, 30, and my husband, 67, began this 2,000-mile trek, nutrition was as important as their other needs. All the best resources we found suggested that caloric intake should be as follows:

- *About half from carbohydrates*
- *About one-quarter from fats*
- *About one-quarter from proteins*

More fats (the foods that tend to be richest in calories) are required in cold weather, when the body burns more calories staying warm. So, in early April, when the wind chill was at times minus-thirty degrees, I loaded extra fats into their diet in the form of peanut butter, margarine, and chocolate.

The name for the hiker snack called "Gorp" originally stood for "Good Old Raisins and Peanuts." Over time, variations of this snack mix developed. We used several varieties of this that the hikers nibbled on during the day to keep their energy levels up.

Greens were never included in food packages, so the hikers had to rely on an occasional restaurant meal in town or a tossed-salad package from the produce department of a grocery. Many hikers supplement that by taking vitamins during their hike.

Don't be concerned about high-sodium foods. Hikers sweat with exertion so much, even in cold weather, that they lose salts from body-water loss. Some of our sources recommended that extra salt or salt tablets be taken when dizziness or light-headedness is experienced in hot weather though others thought that was a bad idea. Powdered drinks such as Gatorade have salts and electrolytes in them. But, be careful: Know the signs of heat stress. Sometimes you just have to stop walking until your body recovers, or you risk heat stroke or heat exhaustion.

Food Preparation

Our hikers found it advantageous to alternate the cooking duties, giving each a day off while the other took his turn. By hiking as a pair and sharing equipment, they needed only one stove, one fuel unit, one set of cooking utensils, one water filter, and one collapsible water bag. That meant less equipment to carry, which made it easier to pack more food and resupply less often.

Cooking Equipment

After checking out various backpacking stoves, our hikers decided on the Gaz "Bluet" model. It proved to be very reliable, except when the temperature dropped below freezing. This stove burns fuel from a butane or butane–propane cartridge. They chose it because its sealed fuel cartridges could be mailed legally, as long as they were not sent by air mail. Flammable fluids, such as "white gas" (also called Coleman fuel), cannot be shipped.

Despite our success with the Gaz, you should know that many other A.T. hikers prefer using white gas, which burns hotter and cooks faster, especially in cold weather. Hikers refill fuel bottles along the way in towns, at hostels, and at camping stores. With white gas, you can also share fuel in a pinch; the issue of disposing of used-up cartridges is not a factor. You should consider whether you prefer a butane stove that simmers well and is less likely to scorch or a white-gas stove that cooks faster and hotter and does not need to be pampered in freezing weather.

Generally, we figured that a Gaz cartridge would cook seven meals. To extend the life of the cartridge, Alan and Dan would bring food to a boil, then remove the covered pan from the heat and cover it with a towel or jacket, so that the food continued to cook for several more minutes. This method also worked for cooking two foods at a time: covering one pot with a towel or jacket while other food or water was on the stove.

Always use a lid when cooking. It makes the contents heat more quickly, keeps them warmer longer, and saves fuel. Another hint is to add dried ingredients before the water comes to a boil, ignoring instructions on prepackaged food that say to bring it to a boil first. The less time it takes to cook a dish, the longer the fuel will last, and the less you have to carry.

Our hikers began the Appalachian Trail on April 1 at Springer Mountain in Georgia. On the cold nights in early April, they found the Gaz stove operated better if they put the canister between their sleeping bags at night for extra warmth before bringing it out to cook.

One-pot meals are often the most convenient for thru-hikers.

Cooking Equipment Used

Here is what they carried to prepare their meals:

- ☐ *1½-quart stainless-steel saucepan and lid*
- ☐ *1-quart stainless-steel saucepan and lid*
- ☐ *Two plastic bowls (former margarine containers)*
- ☐ *Two plastic cups with measuring units marked*

All of the above nested together and fit into a nylon bag. Total weight, including bag, was 24 ounces. Each of them carried a Sierra cup and a Swiss Army knife. In addition, they carried:

- [ ] *One lightweight, Teflon-coated fry pan (handle folded in). (Note: For those using Teflon cookware, do not use sand as a "quick clean" for your pans—it's very destructive.)*
- [ ] *Pancake turner*
- [ ] *Two tablespoons*
- [ ] *One fork*
- [ ] *One plastic picnic knife*
- [ ] *One can opener*

When you decide on your own cooking kit, consider these points: Are the bowls sturdy enough to contain boiling liquids without melting or spilling? Will your cups work equally well for boiling-hot soup and icy water? Do the pans have handles or come with a "pot lifter"? You might prefer to use Lexan spoons and forks, which are sturdy enough not to melt when used to stir boiling foods; many hikers use an all-purpose camping knife rather than bringing a separate cooking knife.

Many "ultralightweight" hikers carry only a single cookpot, spoon, and knife and plan a menu of quick, one-pot meals. We thought that this would become monotonous during a long hike and packed more.

2 Ingredients and Staples

Most food, including fruits, vegetables, and meats, can be dried.
Once the water is removed, foods become light enough to carry in a backpack and will survive the heat, cold, rain, and constant jostling of a thru-hike. Consequently, most of the foods we prepared for mail drops were dried or dehydrated, but not all.

Dried Foods

These days, if you live near a city, you can probably buy most of the dried foods you'll want on a hike at a natural-foods store, specialty-foods store, or backpacking store. But, if you need these foods in quantity, as thru-hikers do, that can get very expensive. One good alternative to buying dried foods is using a food dehydrator, many brands of which are available at quite reasonable prices. Even more economical is the in-stove method that we used. We started by drying foods and testing recipes for quantity, flavor, cooking time, and preparation time.

Among the ingredients we dried were the following:

APPLES—In November, we began drying apple rings strung up over the wood stove. We dried one-and-a-half bushels of Ida Red apples, which was just about right for the duration of the hike. Each medium apple was peeled, cored, sliced into five or six slices, and dipped in bottled lemon juice. Then, it was strung up between ceiling beams near the wood stove (but not directly over it). Drying usually took about three days, until the slices were pliable but not brittle and could be sealed in zip-closure bags.

PEARS AND PINEAPPLE RINGS—Canned pineapple rings and canned pear pieces dried in a dehydrator both proved successful. Pineapple rings, in particular, turned out to be quite a favorite on the Trail. My son was then living in Minneapolis and had access to a dehydrator. He watched for sales on cans of pineapple rings—the best sales were during the holiday season. He emptied many cans, drying the fruit and sealing the rings in zip-closure bags after drying.

OTHER FRUITS—We used raisins, pitted prunes (usually four per person), and apricots. Occasionally, we bought a variety box of dried fruits. Those were quite expensive, however, so we did not use them often.

MEATS AND VEGETABLES—Dan dried corn, peas, chicken, and tuna in his dehydrator. The chicken was a favorite and was used many ways. One ounce of dried chicken, rehydrated during cooking on the Appalachian Trail, worked well for recipes that called for a five-ounce can of chicken.

Oven-Dried Vegetables

One of the simplest and most economical ways of drying foods is in the oven. Using our electric oven at the lowest possible setting, I covered each oven shelf with a doubled layer of cheesecloth, spread out sliced celery, sliced carrots or other vegetables in a single layer, and propped open the door an inch or so with a wooden spoon. These would dry overnight (in six to eight hours) and be ready to pack-age in the morning.

Frozen vegetables from the supermarket work well for dehydrating. But, since we had a large supply of home-grown green beans in our freezer, we used those. I dried some for use in stews and one-pot meals. Later, I dried fresh beans from our garden and found them to be tough. I was advised that fresh vegetables should be blanched (dipped in boiling water for one to two minutes) to avoid toughness.

When dried peas are among the ingredients listed in the recipes in Chapter 5, they are referred to as "home-dried peas," so that no one makes the mistake of purchasing the *split peas* commonly used for soups. Split peas require hours to cook. A 16-ounce package of frozen peas can be dried overnight in your oven.

When dried properly, sliced vegetables will have a texture that is leathery rather than brittle; corn and peas will be hard, like pebbles. Just because a food has been dried, however, doesn't mean it will last forever. Dried foods can mildew and decompose if left too long at room temperature or in humid conditions. In order to keep dried food indefinitely, store it in the freezer until you're ready to send it. Then, it should last through the mailing process and for the week or so that it stays in a backpack.

We purchased some already-prepared dried foods, such as mushrooms, tomato flakes, and egg powder. Sources for those items are listed in the appendix. Dried onions were purchased from the bulk-food department of our neighborhood grocery. Dried potatoes were taken from the generic "au gratin" potato packages. Health-food stores, bulk-food pantries, and food coops were excellent sources of recipe items.

Cold-Weather Food

During cold weather, you will want to increase the fats in a hiker's diet. Oils, margarine, nuts, and cheese not only have lots of calories, they are digested slowly and therefore warm the body longer. Peanut butter and chocolate are good cold-weather foods. During cold periods, we were able to ship yeast breads without fear of moldiness. We did so by sending small, unsliced, home-baked loaves; Those that kept well are noted in the recipes in Chapter 5.

Hot-Weather Food

Summer and hot months provide a bit of a challenge when sending perishable food supplies. But, some perishables travel surprisingly well.

BREADS—Breads made with yeast did not hold up, becoming moldy during the week of shipping and a few days on the Trail. I sent a mini-loaf of home-made bread in each of the first few mail drops, but, as soon as the weather got warm, a phone call from the Trail let me know the season for yeast breads was over. Thereafter, we sent only Logan bread or nonyeast breads.

Some store-bought bagels and flour tortillas will last about a week, even in hot weather, if they are purchased by hikers at town stops and immediately taken on the Trail. We didn't use them because they don't work well in mail drops, but many thru-hikers buy them along the way at supermarkets and stores in town. Don't pick the fresh-baked bagels, or the refrigerated or frozen varieties, as they don't stand up to warm-weather conditions well. Pick the pre-packaged ones (with preservatives added) in the bread aisle of the supermarket. Many hikers report that flour tortillas last well in hot weather.

CHEESES—Cheese does surprisingly well on the Trail. I sent packages of cheese (aged cheeses like Cheddar or Swiss) in their original wrappers, usually in eight-ounce or ten-ounce sizes. We found that Monterey Jack cheese keeps very well on the Trail. If I sent shredded cheese, it was in the four-ounce store package. Shredded cheese doesn't last as well,

One-pot dinner ingredients

Meat or Meat Substitute	Pasta/Grains	Vegetables	Soups/Sauces	Seasonings	Toppings
Dried chicken	Spaghetti noodles	Home-dried peas	Dried soup mixes	Salt	Cheese
Dried tuna	Macaroni	Home-dried beans	Dried sauce mixes	Pepper	Nuts
Canned meats	Rice (instant, white, brown, wild)	Home-dried green pepper	Gravy mix	Dried parsley flakes	Coconut
Dried fish	Ramen noodles	Home-dried carrots	Sour cream mix	Garlic powder	Sunflower seeds
Canned fish (tuna, salmon, sardines, crab, shrimp)	Chow mein noodles	Home-dried celery	White sauce	Onion powder	Bacon bits
Dried salmon	Couscous	Home-dried corn	Spaghetti sauce	Curry	Croutons
Pepperoni	Bulgar	Dried mushrooms	Stroganoff mix	Italian seasoning	Dried fruit bits
Chipped beef		Dried tomato flakes	Taco sauce	Poultry seasoning	Nonfat dry milk
Jerky		Dried onion		Oregano	Parmesan cheese
Ground beef (dried)		Dried mashed potatoes		Basil	
TVP (texturized vegetable protein)		Dried sliced potatoes (from generic "au gratin" package)			

however, and, unlike blocks of cheese, you can't cut off the moldy parts. Other hikers have reported success purchasing cream cheese in town before they begin the week's hike, but we never tried mailing it.

OTHER FOODS—As the weather became hotter, we sent "Gorp" and trail mixes that contained chocolate or butterscotch bits less and less frequently. M&Ms replaced them in mixes, or raisins and dates were used with nut mixes. Compared to cold weather, when we had sent Cup-A-Soup mixes as a camp "pick-me-up," in the summer we sent malted-milk mix that they could add to cold water.

One-Pot Substitutions

Many of the recipes in Chapter 5 will work with one pot, but some require two. Since many hikers carry only a single pot to save weight, the table of ingredients on page 14 can help you improvise your own recipes for one-pot meals.

The Final Months

From talking with other long-distance hikers, we've learned that, during the final month or two of a hike, it's especially important to provide a variety of foods and some dishes that the hikers haven't encountered before. After four or five months of Trail food, traditional thru-hiking staples such as Ramen noodles (which Alan and Dan refused to eat), macaroni and cheese, and Lipton Noodles & Sauce become very unpopular. Variety is especially important at this time, and treats are particularly appreciated.

Supplemental Foods

Sometimes Alan and Dan supplemented mail drops with food that they bought at supermarkets along the way. Often these were heavier items that violated lightweight-back-packing principles, including canned foods that they used to add additional protein or fresh vegetables. Our hikers added such items to the menu for the first few days out of town after a stop. They could include the following:

- *Macaroni and cheese or other packaged dinners*
- *Dinty Moore stew*
- *Cottage cheese*
- *Canned baked beans 'n franks or beans 'n sausages*
- *Spam, canned chicken, or canned tuna (which is now available in lightweight foil packages in most supermarkets)*

- *Green salad (in a cellophane "Fresh Pak")*
- *Instant breakfast cereals (made by adding water and not requiring milk)*

I sometimes included dried milk with "au gratin" potato seasoning packets. This they made into a fondue, with a loaf of French bread and a package of grated cheese that they purchased at a store.

Testing Recipes

As we experimented with recipes, each was tried out in our kitchen for accuracy of ingredients, such as the amount of liquid needed and proper seasoning, and then "taste-approved" by one or both of our hikers. Some of the recipes had been used in previous camp-outs or backpacking trips and only needed to be adjusted to serve two people.

In each of these recipes, cooking time was noted and later tested on the actual camping stove they would use to see how many days of use could be expected from each fuel canister. Alan did a three-day "shakedown" hike with all foods packaged as they would be for the A.T., including cooking instructions. He uncovered a couple of needed changes that weekend.

Dan, who had a heartier appetite, was sent a complete five-day food supply (including Gorp and midafternoon and midmorning snacks) as a test, to see if we should increase portions. He was not to supplement the food package during the five-day test period. Since he was training vigorously for the A.T. hike at this time, we felt it would be a valid test. As expected, we did increase the size of some of the meals.

Variations for the Solo Hiker

If you are planning your own hike and don't have someone at home to prepare your packages as you need them, you will need to have this done in advance. This means your options for what to pack (and what will keep without spoiling) may be more limited, and you'll have to supplement your supplies more often at markets in Trail towns. For example, you may want to substitute *peanut butter and crackers* for *cheese and crackers*. To figure out how long an 18-ounce jar (two cups) of peanut butter will last you, measure out 1/4 cup and test it to see how many lunches you can get out of it and how many crackers you will use per lunch. Calculate the weight of the jar added to the weight of the crackers. To keep your total food weight under the two-pounds-per-day target, add a freeze-dried dinner (which weighs next to nothing) in that same package. For variety, the next package might contain a small plastic container of butter/peanut butter/honey spread. Again, test it to see how many lunches you can anticipate getting out of each container.

Other Tips

When measuring out portions of oatmeal, macaroni and cheese, and other such staples, add more than you would feel comfortable eating at home. Some hikers pack an extra day's food in each shipment in case the store where they had planned to resupply has gone out of business. This also accommodates an increase in appetite after the first few weeks on the Trail.

Consider buying a box of ginger cookies and having your shipper pack in a three-ounce package of cream cheese in an airtight plastic container. (Do make sure of your timing, though, so it won't be waiting for weeks at a post office before you get there.) After opening the airtight package, it should then be good for two to three days. Those cookies become wonderful treats.

3 Mail-Drop List and Schedule

When you start computing your schedule and planning mail drops, it's important to figure out how many miles per day your hikers will travel. Be conservative at first. They may not be in shape to do "big miles," and their appetites may be smaller. Later, once they are fit, they'll start hiking longer days and will need more calories in the food to provide sufficient energy.

By the end of the hike, male hikers in particular may have lost a lot of weight, burning away whatever margin of body fat they had to begin with. Many male hikers lose between twenty-five and fifty pounds during a thru-hike (women tend not to lose as much weight), so it's very important in the final few months of the hike to include high-calorie, high-protein menus that will provide the energy needed to finish.

Where to Send Mail Drops

You can send your mail drops to any post office near the Trail. If you make advance arrangements, you may also be able to send them to camping stores, hostels, motels, and other businesses. Those may be open at more convenient hours than post offices, especially on weekends. Here's what the *Appalachian Trail Thru-Hike Planner* says:

> Many thru-hikers send between 12 and 18 mail drops; one sent himself 30. The factors involved are: How much resupplying you will do from mail drops, and how often you want to go into town for foodstuffs.
>
> A good rule of thumb is: Don't send yourself a mail drop to a town farther than one mile off the Trail unless you were planning to stop there anyway.... It's annoying to walk in and out of a town solely for a mail drop.

Preparing Your Mail Drop

Collect and sort your mail drops before you go. If you don't have anyone sending provisions, as I did for Alan and Dan, go ahead and pack and label the boxes before you leave. Don't seal them, in case you need to add something. And, don't forget nonfood items, such as travelers checks, stamps, and so forth. The ATC's *Thru-Hike Planner* gives more complete and exact information about which nonfood items are commonly included in mail drops.

My list of things to add to the drop included:

☐ *Maps for upcoming sections*
☐ *Pages torn from Appalachian Trail guidebooks*
☐ *Eight stamped envelopes per package*
☐ *Ten stamps for postcards*
☐ *Camera film*
☐ *Butane fuel canister*
☐ *Toilet paper (flattened half-rolls saved in advance)*
☐ *Squeeze Parkay margarine*
☐ *Extra tape and brown paper for mailing items back (such as exposed film, food bags, and seasonal clothing or gear)*
☐ *Small bottle of biodegradable soap or cleaner*

Additional items you might wish to add are:

☐ *Vitamins for the number of days until the next package*
☐ *Refills and replacement for first-aid items*
☐ *Refills and replacement for toiletry items*
☐ *Extra socks or underwear*
☐ *Matches or lighter, candles*
☐ *Extra salt, spices, dried milk*

Our dining room became a major stockroom and shipping room. There were stacks of map pages and Trail-guide pages with labels to ship to the specific addresses.

Packages were insured and shipped Priority Mail allowing about a week for arrival. If you're shipping approved butane canisters, they must be sent by slower surface mail, which means allowing for additional shipping time. As in the following example, a North Carolina town in the spring, we addressed them using the hikers' real names, not the "Trail names" that some hikers use:

Alan or Dan Adsmond
General Delivery
Hot Springs, NC 28743
Please hold for Northbound Appalachian Trail Hiker,
due 4/27

Mail Drop Schedule

The table on the following pages shows where we sent mail drops (using mileages then). You will probably decide on a different schedule based on your start date and expected daily mileage. In between are towns or road crossings at which additional supplies can be purchased or where additional mail drops can be shipped. A list of post offices commonly used by thru-hikers is included on pages 114–120 of this book. Addresses for businesses or hostels that accept mail-drop packages are available in the *Thru-Hikers' Companion*, published annually by the Appalachian Trail Conservancy and Appalachian Long Distance Hikers Association. Mileage there is correct as of January 2009.

It's not immediately apparent, but our schedule also

Hot Springs, North Carolina. Many post offices along the A.T. are in small towns, with limited hours.

allowed for some days off the Trail. It's a good idea to plan some into yours.

Remember that many of the post offices are in out-of-the-way towns, and some of the smaller ones keep irregular hours. Make sure that you allow enough time for your packages to arrive and that your hikers can get to town by closing time, Monday–Saturday, in order to pick them up. If they can't, you might consider sending packages to a Trail-oriented business or hiker hostel in the area.

Mail-Drop Schedule

Pick-up Date	Resupply Location	Meals Prepared	Days Before Next Mail Drop	Miles to Hike
April 1	**Transported to Springer Mountain** (start of A.T.)	Food for 4 days	4 days	30.7
April 4	**Neels Gap, Georgia,** UPS only *Possible interim resupply at Wallace Gap, North Carolina (76.6 miles north of Neels Gap); camp store 1 mile off Trail*	Food for 6 days	10 days	107.0
April 14	**Wesser, North Carolina**	Food for 3 days	3 days	27.6
April 17	**N.C. 28, Fontana Dam, North Carolina,** PO 2 miles off Trail *Possible interim resupply at U.S. 221, Newfound Gap (41.7 miles north of Fontana Dam); ride required* *Possible interim resupply at Davenport Gap, North Carolina (73 miles north of Fontana Dam); camp store 1 mile off Trail*	Food for 5 days	10 days	108.8
April 27	**Hot Springs, North Carolina** *Possible interim resupply at Erwin, Tennessee (67.8 miles north of Hot Springs)*	Food for 6 days	11 days	142.5
May 8	**U.S. 321, Hampton, Tennessee,** PO 1.8 miles off Trail	Food for 3 days	3 days	41.7

Pick-up Date	Resupply Location	Meals Prepared	Days Before Next Mail Drop	Miles to Hike
May 11	**Damascus, Virginia**	Food for 4 days	8 days	152.3
	Possible interim resupply at Va. 16 (63.8 miles north of Damascus); ride required		*(9 days if to Pearisburg)*	*(162.3 if to Pearisburg)*
	Possible interim resupply at U.S. 21/52 (120.4 miles north of Damascus); ride required			
May 19	**Sugar Run Gap** *(Note: Hostel open only May–July; at other times, send mail drop to Pearisburg, 10 miles north on A.T.)*	Food for 5 days	14 days	224.2 miles
	Possible interim resupply at Pearisburg, Virginia (10 miles north of Sugar Run Gap)		*(13 if from Pearisburg)*	*(214.2 if from Pearisburg)*
	Possible interim resupply at Catawba, Virginia (71.4 miles north of Pearisburg)			
	Possible interim resupply at Daleville, Virginia (101.0 miles north of Pearisburg)			
	Possible interim resupply at US 501 (147.4 miles north of Pearisburg), ride required			
June 2	**U.S. 250, Rockfish Gap, Virginia,** PO at Waynesboro; ride required	Food for 6 days	14 days	162.8 miles
	Possible interim resupply in Shenandoah National Park waysides during summers			
	Possible interim resupply at U.S. 522, Front Royal, Virginia (106.9 miles north of Rockfish Gap); ride required			

Pick-up Date	Resupply Location	Meals Prepared	Days Before Next Mail Drop	Miles to Hike
June 16	**Harpers Ferry, West Virginia** *Possible interim resupply at Boiling Springs, Pennsylvania (97.4 miles north of Harpers Ferry)*	Food for 6 days	10 days	123.1 miles
June 26	**Duncannon, Pennsylvania**	Food for 4 days	4 days	69.9 miles
June 30	**Port Clinton, Pennsylvania** *Possible interim resupply at Pa. 873, Palmerton, Pennsylvania (40.1 miles north of Port Clinton); ride required*	Food for 6 days	8 days	76.5 miles
July 8	**Delaware Water Gap, Pennsylvania** *Possible interim resupply at Glenwood, New Jersey (61.8 miles north of Delaware Water Gap), 1.1 miles off Trail*	Food for 5 days	7 days	109.2 miles
July 15	**Bear Mountain, New York** *Possible interim resupply at Kent, Connecticut (64.5 miles north of Bear Mountain), 0.8 mile off Trail* *Possible interim resupply at Salisbury, Connecticut (98 miles north of Bear Mountain)*	Food for 3 days	13 days	167.2 miles

Pick-up Date	Resupply Location	Meals Prepared	Days Before Next Mail Drop	Miles to Hike
July 28	**Dalton, Massachusetts**	Food for 6 days	8 days	131.5 miles
	Possible interim resupply at Vt. 11/30, Manchester Center, Vermont (81.8 miles north of Dalton); ride required.			
August 5	**Killington, Vermont,** PO 2.2 miles off the Trail; ride required	Food for 3 days	4 days	45.1 miles
August 9	**Hanover, New Hampshire**	Food for 5 days	8 days	122.9 miles
	Possible interim resupply at U.S. 3, North Woodstock, New Hampshire (69.2 miles north of Hanover); ride required.			
August 17	**N.H. 16, Pinkham Notch Camp,** UPS packages only	Food for 4 days	6 days	62.5 miles
	Possible interim resupply at US 2, Gorham, New Hampshire (20.1 miles north of Pinkham Notch); ride required.			
August 23	**East B Hill Road, Andover, Maine,** PO 8 miles off the Trail, ride required.	Food for 5 days	6 days	68.7 miles
	Possible interim resupply at Maine 4, Rangeley, Maine (36. 5 miles north of Andover); ride required			
August 29	**Maine 27, Stratton, Maine,** PO 5 miles off the Trail, ride required	Food for 5 days	5 days	70 miles
	Possible interim mail drop at U.S. 201, Caratunk, Maine (36.6 miles north of Stratton), 0.3 miles off the Trail			
September 3	**Monson, Maine,** PO 2 miles off the Trail.	Food for 10 days	9 days	117.8 miles

4 Menus

Here are actual menus that we used for Alan and Dan's thru-hike. You can use them simply as a guide, adding your own variations, or you can follow our recommendations in detail. As the table in Chapter 3 shows, not all the packages took our hikers through to the next mail-drop location. In many instances, they resupplied at towns along the way and treated themselves to restaurant food. Menu items in **bold** are included in the recipe section in Chapter 5.

Packaging

We "color-coordinated" our food bags in nylon drawstring bags. When a six-day package went out, breakfasts were in a red bag, lunches in a green bag, and dinners in a blue bag. Each time our hikers picked up a new bag, they'd mail the old one back.

BREAKFAST—All cereals included:

- *Dried milk necessary for the meal*
- *Herbal tea bag (to be shared) or*
- *Hot-chocolate packets*

Breakfast bags also included the morning snack (such as Gorp). On a six-day resupply, to cut down on weight, we'd empty a foil package of Carnation Instant Breakfast into a plastic sandwich bag and add dried milk, directions, and a label. We'd close these with a twist-tie and cut off any excess from the bag before slipping them into a zip-closure bag with the other breakfast offerings and morning snack. Six of those zipped bags went into the red breakfast bag.

Their favorite breakfast was a mix of one package of Instant Cream of Wheat with one package of strawberry-flavored Carnation Instant Breakfast. I included it in almost every food pacakge. It was quick and easy, and they could start hiking in no time. Sometimes thay would get up at 5 a.m. and hike a couple of hours before breakfast.

LUNCH—Lunches included afternoon snacks, so they would be handy after lunch without further searching through packs. During hot weather, we included a package of Kool-Aid to add to their water bottles. Flavored drinks such as Kool-Aid or Gatorade encouraged our hikers to drink more often, helping them stay hydrated. They also improve the taste of iodine-treated water.

DINNER—Dinner bags were a little larger. They typically included:

- *One Lipton Cup-A-Soup or*
- *A malted-milk mix, as a hot-weather energy pick-up while dinner was being prepared*
- *Tea bags or coffee packets*

BEDTIME SNACK—Last but not least for our hikers was the bedtime snack of a Tiger's Milk Bar (one of several different flavors). They seemed to enjoy them so much that we included them with every dinner package.

The norm seems to be that thru-hikers lose large amounts of weight. Our hikers were thin to begin with and could ill afford to lose more. Actually, each gained five pounds over the course of the 2,160 miles. They give credit to the Tiger's Milk Bars.

1 Carried to Dahlonega — WINTER

Day 1 [Restaurant—Dahlonega]

SNACK **Gorp #2**

Wheat crackers, mild cheddar cheese, dried apples, **Hiker's Bars**

SNACK **Gorp #2**

Ham slices, Lipton Noodles & Sauce (Alfredo), **Logan Bread**

Day 2 **Cream of Wheat Cereal** with hot water, dried meat stick

SNACK **Joe Frogger Cookies** (4" size)

Swiss cheese, rye crackers, dried apricots, **Joe Frogger Cookies**

SNACK **Joe Frogger Cookies**

Beef-mushroom Rice-a-Roni, **Swedish Limpa Bread,** lime Jell-O (hot)

Day 3 Instant Cream of Wheat with strawberry Instant Breakfast, Smoky Links (1/2 package)

SNACK **Trail mix**

Swiss cheese, rye crackers, dried apricots, **Yum Balls**

SNACK **Trail mix**

Freeze-dried chicken stew, **Honey Bread,** brownies

Day 4 Instant grits, Smoky Links (1/2 package), hot chocolate

SNACK **Gorp #1**

Potted ham spread, cornmeal rounds, prunes
(4 each), granola bars

SNACK **Gorp #1**

[Restaurant—Neels Gap]

2 Neels Gap to Wesser   WINTER

Day 1 **Sunrise Spuds**, hot chocolate

SNACK **Gorp #8**

Oat crisps, ham spread, dried pineapple, **Anzacs**

SNACK **Gorp #8**

Chicken Rice Curry, **Logan Bread**

Day 2 Strawberry Instant Breakfast, Grape Nuts and milk,
Logan Bread

SNACK Beef sticks

Cheddar cheese, sesame rye crackers, dried apples,
Sunbelt bar

SNACK Nutrilite bar

Isle Royale Dinner, brownies, peppermint tea

Day 3 **Scrambled Eggs**, breakfast bar

SNACK **Gorp #5**

Peanut butter, wheat crackers, dried apples,
granola bars

SNACK **Gorp #5**

Freeze-dried beef stew, **7-Grain Bread**, pistachio
pudding

Day 4 Instant grits, lime Jell-O (hot), **7-Grain Bread**
(left-over)

SNACK **Yum Balls**

Summer sausage (1/2 roll), snack crackers,
dried apricots, granola bars

SNACK **Gorp #5**

Expedition Spaghetti, oat bread and butter, **Gorp #5**

Day 5 **Granola** (1 cup), dried milk (1/3 cup) each

SNACK **Gorp #6**

Peanut butter, oat crisps, dried pineapple, granola bars

SNACK **Gorp #6**

Corn Chowder, oat bread, **Anzacs**

Day 6 **Instant Oatmeal**, **Honey Bread**

SNACK **Beef Jerky**

Summer sausage ($^1/_2$ roll), snack crackers, **Peanut-Butter Balls**

SNACK **Beef Jerky**

Vegetarian Stew, **Carrot Cake**

3 Wesser to Fontana Dam   WINTER

Day 1 **Instant Oatmeal**, **Peanut-Butter Balls**

SNACK **Gorp #5**

Swiss cheese, wheat crackers, dried apples, snack bar

SNACK **Gorp #5**

Shrimp Rice Dinner, Buckwheat Bread, brownies

Day 2 **Muesli**, prunes

SNACK Chocolate bar

Cheddar cheese, oat crackers, dried pineapple, snack bar

SNACK **Beef Jerky**

Chicken Klister with Peas, Camper's Bread, **Peanut-Butter Balls**

Day 3 **Sunrise Spuds**, hot chocolate

SNACK **Gorp #7**

Monterey Jack cheese, rye crackers, dried apples, granola bar

SNACK **Gorp #7**

Gran-burger (4 packs ketchup), wheat buns, mashed potatoes, gravy packet, hot chocolate

4 Fontana Dam to Hot Springs   WINTER

Day 1 **Ralston Cereal** with nuts

SNACK **Gorp #4**

Peanut butter, graham crackers, dried apple, **Yum Balls**

SNACK **Gorp #4**

Isle Royale Dinner, Congo Bars

Day 2 **Granola**, 2 meat sticks, lime Jell-O (hot)

SNACK **Trail Mix**

Pepperoni slices ($^1/_2$ package), snack crackers, **Trail Mix**, dried pineapple

SNACK Nutrilite bar

Chipped Beef Stew, Honey Bread

Day 3   **Scrambled Eggs, Logan Bread,** Ovaltine

SNACK Cinnamon grahams

Pepperoni slices (½ package), snack crackers, **Gorp #5,** dried apples

SNACK **Gorp #8**

Chicken Stew, mashed potatoes, **Zucchini Bread,** pistachio pudding

Day 4   Instant Cream of Wheat with strawberry Instant Breakfast, breakfast bars

SNACK **Gorp #3**

Vienna sausages, wheat crackers, dried pineapple

SNACK **Gorp #3**

Cup-A-Soup, **Chipped Beef and Broccoli Dish, Logan Bread,** strawberry bars

Day 5   Instant oat bran, **Honey Bread**

SNACK **Trail Mix**

Cheddar cheese, Triscuits, apricots, chewy granola bars

SNACK **Beef Jerky**

[Restaurant—Hot Springs]

5   Hot Springs to Hampton   SPRING

Day 1   **Sunrise Spuds,** hot chocolate

SNACK **Trail Mix**

7-grain crackers, ham spread, dried pineapple, chocolate chip bars

SNACK **Trail Mix**

Chicken Curry, 7-Grain Bread, lime Jell-O (hot)

Day 2   Instant grits, lime Jell-O (hot), **7-Grain Bread** (leftover)

SNACK **Gorp #5**

Graham crackers with **Honey/Butter/Peanut Butter** spread, dried apples, **Hiker's Bars**

SNACK **Gorp #5**

Manhattan Clam Chowder, 7-Grain Bread, Fudge Scotch Squares

Day 3   Grape Nuts and milk, **Logan Bread**

SNACK Peanuts

Brown rice snack thins, cheddar cheese, prunes, granola bars

SNACK Peanuts

Tuna Helper with dried tuna, **Logan Bread,** banana pudding

Day 4   **Muesli, Logan Bread**

SNACK **Beef Jerky**

Swiss cheese, oat crisp, dried apples, chewy fruit bar

SNACK Mixed nuts

Isle Royale Chicken, Camper's Bread**,** butterscotch fudge

Day 5   **Scrambled Eggs**, breakfast bar

SNACK **Gorp #6**

Honey/Butter/Peanut Butter spread, snack crackers, dried apples, date-nut bars

SNACK **Gorp #6**

Lentil soup (packet) with cocktail sausages, **Kasha,** zucchini bars

Day 6   **Granola**, Sunbelt Bar

SNACK Sunflower seeds

Cheddar cheese, snack crackers, apricots, granola bars

SNACK **Beef Jerky**

Expedition Spaghetti, Logan Bread, semisweet chocolate squares

Day 1   **Sunrise Spuds,** hot chocolate

SNACK **Gorp #1**

Honey/Butter/Peanut Butter spread, wheat crackers, dried apples, **Fudge Scotch Squares**

SNACK **Trail mix**

Corn Chowder, Logan Bread (Apple flavor), vanilla pudding with nuts

Day 2   **Granola, Choco-Camp Bread**

SNACK Peanuts

Swiss cheese, crackers, apricots, chewy granola bars

SNACK **Gorp #5**

African Peanut Stew, Choco-Camp Bread, lime Jell-O (hot)

Day 3   Instant grits, prunes, granola bar

SNACK Sunflower seeds

Honey/Butter/Peanut Butter spread, wheat crackers, dried apples, **Congo Bars**

SNACK Peanuts

Shrimp Rice Dinner, Logan Bread (apple flavor), **Hiker's Bars**, Ovaltine (hot)

7   Damascus to Sugar Run Gap   SPRING

Day 1   **Ralston Cereal** with nuts and raisins

SNACK Mixed nuts

Pilot biscuits, ham spread, dried apples, **Congo Bars**

SNACK **Trail Mix**

Top Shelf Dinners, **Logan Bread**

Day 2   Instant grits, meat sticks (2)

SNACK **Gorp #5**

Cheddar-cheese snack crackers, dried pineapple, chewy granola bar

SNACK **Gorp #5**

Chicken Stew, mashed potatoes, butterscotch pudding

Day 3   Oatmeal with raisins and banana chips

SNACK Mixed nuts

Monterey Jack cheese, wheat crackers, prunes, butterscotch bars

SNACK Peanuts

Chicken Polynesian with rice, Camper's Bread

Day 4   **Scrambled Eggs, Logan Bread,** hot chocolate

SNACK **Trail mix**

Swiss cheese, oat crisp, dried apples, granola bar

SNACK **Trail mix**

Chili-To-Go, Lipton Noodles & Sauce (alfredo), **Carrot Cake**

8   Sugar Run Gap to Waynesboro   SPRING

Day 1   **Granola, Peanut-Butter Balls**

SNACK sunflower seeds

Honey/Butter/Peanut Butter spread, crackers, dried apples, **Hiker's Bars**

SNACK **Gorp #8**

Fontana Dinner, Logan Bread, candy canes

Day 2   Pancakes with instant maple syrup, meat sticks

SNACK **Gorp #8**

Pepperoni slices (½ package), snack crackers, **Trail Mix**, dried pineapple

SNACK **Beef Jerky**

St. Patrick's Stew, Honey Bread, butterscotch pudding with nuts

Day 3 **Scrambled Eggs, Hash Brown Potatoes**

SNACK Beef sticks

Honey/Butter/Peanut Butter spread,
graham crackers, dried apples, Nutrilite bars

SNACK **Gorp #7**

**Turkey Trail Dinner, Spotted Applesauce,
Honey Bread**

Day 4 **Ralston Cereal** with raisins and nuts

SNACK **Gorp #8**

Pepperoni slices (1/2 package), snack crackers, apricots,
Sunbelt bar

SNACK **Gorp #8**

Instant broccoli soup, **Chicken Rag-Out**, Lipton
Noodles & Sauce (sour cream and chives), **Carrot Cake**

Day 5 Instant Cream of Wheat with strawberry Instant
Breakfast, breakfast bars

SNACK **Trail Mix**

Cheddar cheese, wheat crackers, prunes, brownies

SNACK **Trail Mix**

Chipped Beef and Broccoli Dish, **Logan Bread**,
lime Jell-O (hot)

---

9   **Waynesboro to Harpers Ferry**   SPRING

Day 1 **Granola, Peanut-Butter Balls**

SNACK **Trail Mix**

Sausage chub, snack crackers, raisins, granola bars

SNACK **Trail Mix**

St. Patrick's Stew, Honey Bread, Sesame Balls

Day 2 **Scrambled Eggs**, bagels

SNACK **Gorp #5**

Ham spread, corn crackers, dried apples, **Peanut-
Butter Balls**

SNACK **Gorp #5**

Shrimp Rice Dinner, Logan Bread (apple flavor),
trail bars

Day 3 **Sunrise Spuds,** hot chocolate

SNACK **Beef Jerky**

Cheddar cheese, wheat crackers, dried peaches, fruit bar

SNACK Mixed nuts

**African Peanut Stew, Logan Bread, Spotted
Applesauce**

Day 4   Grape Nuts and milk, breakfast bar

SNACK **Trail Mix**

Peanut butter, snack crackers, dried apples, almond bars

SNACK **Trail Mix**

Chicken Rag-Out, Lipton Noodles & Sauce (sour cream and chives), candy canes

Day 5   **Muesli, Peanut-Butter Balls**

SNACK **Beef Jerky**

Colby cheese, rye crackers, dried pineapple, macaroon bars

SNACK Mixed nuts

Corn Chowder, Swedish Limpa Bread, no-bake cheesecake

Day 6   Instant Cream of Wheat with strawberry Instant Breakfast, breakfast bars

SNACK **Gorp #1**

Peanut butter, snack crackers, apricots, **Yum Balls**

SNACK **Gorp #8**

Mountain House beef stew (freeze-dried), banana cream pudding

Day 1   Instant Cream of Wheat with strawberry Instant Breakfast

SNACK **Trail mix**

Cheddar cheese, snack crackers, dried apples, **Mountain Bars**

SNACK **Trail mix**

Chicken Klister, **Pumpkin Bread**, **Coconut Balls**

Day 2   Instant grits, **Choco-Camp Bread**

SNACK **Gorp #8**

Honey/Butter/Peanut Butter spread, graham crackers, dried pineapple, Nutrilite bar

SNACK **Gorp #8**

Beef Stroganoff, Date-Nut Bread

Day 3   **Scrambled Eggs, Logan Bread,** hot chocolate

SNACK **Gorp #1**

Colby cheese, wheat crackers, apricots, granola bars

SNACK **Gorp #1**

Chicken Curry, Logan Bread, peanut crisps

Day 4   **Granola**, meat sticks (2)

SNACK Salted peanuts

Honey/Butter/Peanut Butter spread, graham crackers, dried apples, **Hiker's Bars**

SNACK Salted peanuts

Richmoor beef burgundy (freeze-dried), **Logan Bread**

Day 5   Instant oat bran with nuts and dried fruit

SNACK **Beef Jerky**

Sardines (can), crackers, dried apples, honey-nut bars

SNACK Licorice sticks

Chicken Stew with Mashed Potatoes, Health Bread, apricot bars

Day 6   Apple-cinnamon oat bran, **Peanut-Butter Balls**

SNACK **Gorp #7**

Swiss cheese, oat crisps, dried pineapple, fig bars

SNACK **Gorp #7**

Spanish Rice/Isle Royale Dinner, Date-Nut Bread, mini-bag of candy corn

Day 1   Prunes, instant grits, **Poppy-seed Bread**

SNACK **Beef Jerky**

Peanut butter and jelly, crackers, dried apples, granola bar

SNACK **Gorp #1**

Nature's Hamburgers, bun, ketchup, mashed potatoes with brown gravy, **Congo Bars**

Day 2   **Instant Oatmeal, Peanut-Butter Balls**

SNACK **Gorp #7**

Smoked oysters (can), wheat crackers, apricots, **Mountain Bars**

SNACK **Gorp #7**

Chipped Beef and Broccoli Dish, Pumpkin Bread, Wheat Chex party mix

Day 3   Instant Cream of Wheat with strawberry Instant Breakfast, breakfast bars (2)

SNACK Animal crackers

Peanut butter and jelly, crackers, dried apples, granola bar

SNACK Animal crackers

Chipped Beef Stew, Logan Bread, Coconut Balls

Day 4   **Cream of Wheat** with dates

SNACK Salted peanuts

Cheddar cheese, wheat crackers, dried pineapple, brownies

SNACK Salted peanuts

Tuna (dried) with Tuna Helper, **Choco-Camp Bread,** Wheat Chex party mix

12   Port Clinton to Delaware Water Gap   SUMMER

Day 1   Pancakes with powdered maple syrup

SNACK **Gorp #7**

Deviled ham spread, melba toast, dried pears, **Fudge Scotch Squares**

SNACK **Gorp #7**

Chicken Stew, Hash Brown Potatoes, bran bars

Day 2   **Instant Oatmeal** with raisins and nuts, **Peanut-Butter Balls**

SNACK **Beef Jerky**

Swiss cheese, rye crackers, **Joe Frogger Cookies,** lemonade

SNACK **Trail mix**

Fontana Dinner, Mountain Bars, astronaut ice cream

Day 3   **Granola**, Sunbelt Bar

SNACK **Trail mix**

Cheddar cheese, crackers, apricots, **Hiker's Bars**

SNACK Peanuts

Expedition Spaghetti, Logan Bread, peppermint treats

Day 4   **Scrambled Eggs, Peanut-Butter Balls**

SNACK **Yum Balls**

Colby cheese, crackers, apricots, **Hiker's Bars**

SNACK **Gorp #5**

Tuna (dried) with Tuna Helper, **Health Bread,** Lemon pudding

Day 5   Instant rice with cinnamon and nutmeg

SNACK **Gorp #5**

Peanut butter, saltines, prunes, raisin cookies

SNACK Mixed nuts

Corn Chowder, Date-Nut Bread, Coconut Balls

Day 6 **Instant Oatmeal**, **Logan Bread**

SNACK **Gorp #4**

Peanut butter, cinnamon grahams, dried apples,
chocolate chip cookies

SNACK **Gorp #4**

Safari Surprise, Logan Bread, peanut crisps

13 Delaware Water Gap to Bear Mountain   SUMMER

Day 1 Instant Cream of Wheat with strawberry Instant
Breakfast, breakfast bars

SNACK **Trail mix**

Sardines (can), crackers, dried apples, Power Bars

SNACK Pumpkin seeds

Hawaiian Chicken, Health Bread, fudge bars

Day 2 Instant oat bran, **Honey Bread**

SNACK **Gorp #7**

Cheddar cheese, wheat crackers, fruit leather, fig bars

SNACK **Gorp #7**

**Chipped Beef with Peas and Mashed Potatoes,
Date-Nut Bread,** peppermint candies

Day 3 Strawberry Instant Breakfast, Grape Nuts and powdered
milk, **Logan Bread**

SNACK **Beef jerky**

Salami chub ($\frac{1}{2}$), snack crackers, fruit leather,
Hiker's Bars

SNACK Peanuts

Chipped Beef Stew, Pumpkin Bread, Sesame Balls

Day 4 Instant grits, Pop Tarts

SNACK **Gorp #5**

Salami chub ($\frac{1}{2}$), oat krisps, dried pineapple,
Scotch Squares

SNACK **Gorp #5**

Tuna with Creamy Noodles, **Health Bread,**
butterscotch pudding and nuts

Day 5 **Granola**, meat sticks (2)

SNACK Mixed nuts

Swiss cheese, wheat crackers, prunes, peanut crisps

SNACK Mixed nuts

Camper's Lentil Stew, Date-Nut Bread, peanut brittle

14   Bear Mountain to Dalton   SUMMER

Day 1   **Instant Oatmeal, Choco-Camp Bread**

SNACK **Gorp #6**

Honey/Butter/Peanut Butter spread, crackers, dried apples, almond bars

SNACK **Gorp #6**

Shrimp-Rice Dinner, Health Bread

Day 2   Instant Cream of Wheat with strawberry Instant Breakfast, breakfast bars

SNACK Peanuts

Colby cheese, wheat crackers, dried pineapple, macaroon bars

SNACK Cracker-Jack

Top Shelf Dinner (chicken), Lipton Noodles & Sauce (alfredo), **Logan Bread, Sesame Balls**

Day 3   **Cream of Wheat** (cinnamon-apple), **Logan Bread**

SNACK Mixed nuts

Honey/Butter/Peanut Butter spread, graham crackers, trail bars

SNACK Mixed nuts

White Mountain Stew, Honey Bread, trail bars

15   Dalton to Killington   SUMMER

Day 1   **Scrambled Eggs, Logan Bread**

SNACK **Trail Mix**

Peanut butter, graham crackers, dried apples, lemonade, fig bars

SNACK **Trail mix**

Corn Chowder, Logan Bread, no-bake cheesecake, Ovaltine

Day 2   Prunes, Grape Nuts cereal, **Peanut-Butter Balls**

SNACK **Gorp #2**

Cheddar Cheese, wheat crackers, dried pineapple, trail bars

SNACK **Gorp #2**

Chicken Rice Curry, Health Bread, 6-layer bars

Day 3   Pancakes with powdered maple syrup, meat stick

SNACK **Joe Frogger Cookies**

Salami chub, wheat crackers, apricots, toffee bars

SNACK **Joe Frogger Cookies**

Oxtail soup cup, **Isle Royale Dinner, Choco-Camp Bread,** lime Jell-O

Day 4 **Granola, Peanut-Butter Balls**

SNACK **Beef Jerky**

Vienna sausage, rye crackers, fruit leather, almond bars

SNACK **Gorp #1**

Camper's Lentil Stew, Honey Bread, pistachio pudding

Day 5 Instant Cream of Wheat with strawberry Instant Breakfast, breakfast bars

SNACK Snack mix

Wheat crackers, cheddar cheese, dried apples, oat bars

SNACK Snack mix

St. Patrick's Stew, Health Bread, strawberry chewy bars

Day 6 **Instant Oatmeal, Honey Bread**

SNACK **Gorp #5**

Peanut butter, snack crackers, fruit leather, granola bars

SNACK **Gorp #5**

Tuna Fettucini, Date Nut Bread, lemon bars

---

16 Killington to Hanover

Day 1 **Instant Oatmeal**, meat sticks

SNACK **Gorp #5**

Salami, crackers, dried apples, granola bar

SNACK **Gorp #5**

Shrimp Rice Dinner, Honey Bread, peanut crisps

Day 2 Prunes, Instant Cream of Wheat with strawberry Instant Breakfast, breakfast bar

SNACK Peanuts

Swiss cheese, wheat crackers, dried pineapple, trail bars

SNACK **Gorp #1**

Chicken Klister, Date-Nut Bread, cherry bars

Day 3 **Muesli, Beef Jerky**

SNACK **Gorp #6**

Colby cheese, rye crackers, fruit leather, almond bar

SNACK **Gorp #6**

Isle Royale Dinner, Logan Bread, Hikers' Bars

Day 1   **Scrambled Eggs, Logan Bread**

SNACK **Joe Frogger Cookies**

Sardines (can), crackers, dried apples, Power Bars

SNACK **Joe Frogger Cookies**

Chipped Beef Stew, Health Bread, no-bake chocolate mint pie

Day 2   Blueberry pancakes with powdered maple syrup, beef sticks

SNACK Snack mix

Cheddar cheese, wheat crackers, fruit leather, fig bars

SNACK Snack mix

Corned beef hash (can) **Hash Brown Potatoes, Logan Bread,** Jell-O

Day 3   Grape Nuts cereal, meat sticks, **Peanut-Butter Balls**

SNACK **Gorp #7**

Salami chub (1/2), snack crackers, fruit leather, **Hiker's Bars**

SNACK **Gorp #7**

Arroz con Queso, taco shells, bran bars

Day 4   **Muesli, Peanut-Butter Balls, Beef Jerky**

SNACK **Gorp #5**

Salami chub (1/2), oat crisps, dried pineapple, **Scotch Squares**

SNACK **Gorp #5**

Chicken Rag-Out, Lipton Noodles & Sauce (sour cream and chives), **Date-Nut Bread**

Day 5   Instant Cream of Wheat with strawberry Instant Breakfast, breakfast bars

SNACK **Gorp #6**

Swiss cheese, wheat crackers, prunes, peanut crisps

SNACK **Gorp #6**

Corn Chowder, Choco-Camp Bread, banana cream pudding

18 Gorham to Andover   FALL

Day 1 **Granola, Peanut-Butter Balls**

SNACK Snack mix

Peanut butter and jelly, snack crackers, dried apples,
Sunbelt Bar

SNACK Snack mix

Broccoli and Chipped Beef Dinner, Health Bread,
no-bake chocolate mousse

Day 2 Pancakes with powdered syrup, meat sticks

SNACK **Gorp #8**

Cheddar cheese, wheat crackers, dried pineapple,
granola bar

SNACK **Gorp #8**

Chipped Beef and Mashed Potatoes, Logan Bread,
peppermint treats

Day 3 Instant grits and dried milk, **Logan Bread**

SNACK **Gorp #5**

Peanut butter and jelly, crackers, dried apples,
Sunbelt Bar

SNACK **Gorp #5**

Corned beef (can), **Hash Brown Potatoes,** Camper's
Bread, **Hiker's Bars**

Day 4 Instant Cream of Wheat with strawberry Instant Breakfast

SNACK Mixed nuts

Salami chub, crackers, dried apples, nutrition bar

SNACK **Beef jerky**

Isle Royale Dinner (with Rice-A-Roni chicken flavor),
Zucchini Bread, coconut pudding

19 Andover to Stratton   FALL

Day 1 Instant Cream of Wheat with strawberry Instant
Breakfast, breakfast bars

SNACK **Trail Mix**

Sardines, crackers, dried pineapple, granola bar

SNACK **Trail Mix**

Shrimp Rice Dinner, Health Bread, coconut cream
pudding

Day 2 Pancakes with powdered maple syrup, beef sticks

SNACK **Gorp #5**

Honey/Butter/Peanut Butter spread, crackers,
dried pineapple, Sunbelt Bar

SNACK **Gorp #5**

Chili-to-Go, Lipton Noodles & Sauce (alfredo), **Zucchini
Bread,** Jell-O (hot)

Day 3 Instant grits, chewy fruit bar

SNACK **Gorp #7**

Swiss cheese, oat crisps, raisins, granola bar

SNACK **Gorp #7**

Malted milk (before dinner), **Camper's Lentil Stew, Honey Bread, Coconut Balls**

Day 4 **Ralston Cereal** with nuts

SNACK **Gorp #5**

Honey/Butter/Peanut Butter spread, graham crackers, dried pineapple, Sunbelt Bar

SNACK **Gorp #5**

Isle Royale Dinner (Rice-a-Roni beef-mushroom flavor), **Choco-Camp Bread**, Wheat Chex party mix

Day 5 **Instant Oatmeal, Peanut-Butter Balls**

SNACK **Gorp #5**

Colby cheese, wheat crackers, prunes, almond bars

SNACK **Gorp #5**

Chicken and Rice Curry, Logan Bread, Sesame Balls

20 Stratton to Monson   FALL

Day 1 **Granola**, meat sticks (2), lime Jell-O (hot)

SNACK **Trail mix**

Cheddar cheese, wheat crackers, dried pineapple, Sunbelt Bar

SNACK **Trail mix**

Tuna Fettucini, Pumpkin Bread, lemon pudding

Day 2 **Scrambled Eggs, Honey Bread**

SNACK **Gorp #2**

Peanut butter, snack crackers, raisins, Sunbelt Bar

SNACK **Gorp #2**

Isle Royale Dinner, Spanish Rice, Honey Bread, Coconut Balls

Day 3 **Cream of Wheat**, prunes

SNACK **Gorp #5**

Vienna sausage, crackers, apricots, granola bar

SNACK **Gorp #5**

White Mountain Stew, Logan Bread, Chinese cookies

Day 4 Instant Cream of Wheat with strawberry Instant Breakfast, breakfast bars

SNACK **Gorp #7**

Peanut butter and jelly, crackers, dried pineapple, **Pecan Crisps**

SNACK **Gorp #7**

Beef Stroganoff, Honey Bread, Mountain Bars

Day 5 Instant apple-cinnamon oat bran, **Logan Bread**

SNACK **Gorp #3**

Swiss cheese, oat crisps, dried apples, fig bars

SNACK **Gorp #3**

Chili-to-Go, Lipton Noodles & Sauce (alfredo), **Health Bread,** pralines

21 Monson to Katahdin   FALL

Day 1 Instant grits, **Peanut-Butter Balls**

SNACK **Trail mix**

Pepperoni slices ($^1/_2$ package), snack crackers, dried apples, granola bar

SNACK **Trail mix**

Deb's African Peanut Stew, Honey Bread, Congo Bars

Day 2 Instant Cream of Wheat with strawberry Instant Breakfast, breakfast bars

SNACK **Gorp #5**

Colby cheese, wheat crackers, dried pineapple, Sunbelt Bar

SNACK **Gorp #5**

Corn Chowder, Honey Bread, Chinese cookies

Day 3 **Granola**, meat sticks

SNACK **Gorp #8**

Pepperoni slices ($^1/_2$ package), snack crackers, fruit leather, Sunbelt Bar

SNACK **Gorp #8**

Chicken and Rice Curry, Health Bread, peppermint candies

Day 4 **Instant Oatmeal**, **Logan Bread**

SNACK **Gorp #8**

Peanut butter and jelly, crackers, dried apples, granola bar

SNACK **Gorp #8**

Tuna-noodle dinner, **Date-Nut Bread,** pralines

Day 5   **Cream of Wheat** (apple-cinnamon), **Logan Bread**
SNACK **Gorp #2**
Peanut butter, crackers, fruit leather, Sunbelt Bar
SNACK **Gorp #2**
White Mountain Stew, Logan Bread, vanilla pudding with nuts

Day 6   Instant Cream of Wheat with strawberry Instant Breakfast, breakfast bars
SNACK **Trail mix**
Cheddar cheese, wheat crackers, dried pineapple, Sunbelt Bar
SNACK **Trail mix**
Chicken Klister, Logan Bread (apple flavor), **Pecan Crisps**

Day 7   Instant grits, **Peanut-Butter Balls**
SNACK **Gorp #5**
Peanut butter, snack crackers, raisins, Sunbelt Bar
SNACK **Gorp #5**
Chili-to-Go, Health Bread, fig bars

Day 8   **Muesli,** meat sticks
SNACK **Gorp #1**
Cheddar cheese, crackers, apricots, granola bars
SNACK **Gorp #1**
St. Patrick's Stew, Honey Bread, Mountain Bars

Day 9   **Instant Oatmeal, Date-Nut Bread**
SNACK Mixed nuts
Honey/Butter/Peanut Butter spread, graham crackers, dried apples, Sunbelt Bar
SNACK Mixed nuts
Isle Royale Dinner, Spanish Rice, Logan Bread, banana cream pudding

Day 10 **Honey Bread**, Instant Oatmeal
SNACK **Beef Jerky**
Honey/Butter/Peanut Butter spread, graham crackers, dried apples, Sunbelt bar
SNACK Peanuts
Curried Vegetables, Logan Bread, Coconut Balls

5 Recipes

Preparing food for the Trail has two phases. The first phase, at home in the kitchen, involves mixing ingredients and preparing packages. In some cases, it also involves Precooking items and baking breads. The second phase is actually cooking the food in camp.

The recipes that follow may include the following elements:

AT-HOME (PREPACKAGING) PREPARATION—cooking and baking ingredients that require advance preparation.

PREHIKE PACKAGING INSTRUCTIONS—Assembling the dried or Precooked ingredients in packages for easy preparation on the trail. Hikers should plan on adding water; some recipes call for bottled margarine (such as Squeeze Parkay) from the week's supply the hikers carry with them.

CAMPSITE COOKING INSTRUCTIONS—Mixing the prepackaged ingredients and preparing them on a camp stove.

To make Trailside cooking easier for the hikers, I included cooking instructions with the packages. I sim-plified the process of making up the food packages by having a sheet of photocopied instructions (both packaging and cooking) on hand. I usually wrote instructions for four or five recipes on a sheet, then just clipped them off as needed, and dropped them in the package. (Even these bits of paper had all margins cut off—not to add more weight than necessary.) For your convenience, in this book we've included campsite cooking instructions on perforated paper that you can tear out and slip in with the food packages. If you plan to use a given recipe more than once, you will need to make some photocopies.

Additional notes can be written on the plastic bag with felt-tip marker. Post-It notes ($1^1/_2$" x 2" size) make handy additions. I constantly clipped any excess tops off sandwich bags, trimmed edges off any packages included—all in the interest of keeping the weight down.

Occasionally, I'd send a can of smoked oysters or sardines, but other foods in that same food drop would have to be extra light (as in a freeze-dried dinner) so that over-all weight did not exceed the two-pounds-per-day limit we sought.

One-Pot Variations

You should become adept at substituting items you may not find in your area by using the table of ingredients for one-pot dinners on page 14 of Chapter 2. To determine amounts and quantities, check some of the other recipes in this chapter and rely on your own preferences to create a new dinner for yourself.

You will find that you get new ideas from your fellow hikers. Some hikers, for instance, report that flour tortillas work well, both as sturdy sandwich containers and as a dinner bread dipped into noodle, bean, and rice dishes.

Some of the items that people have said combine well for one-pot dinners include:

- *Tuna, instant rice, home-dried peas, curry sauce, almonds, and coconut.*
- *Beef jerky bits, ramen noodles, dried tomatoes, dried green pepper, and onion flakes.*
- *Bacon bits, dried potato slices, home-dried green beans, and cheese sauce mix from generic "au gratin" potatoes.*
- *Bulgar, dried corn, dried mushrooms, and stroganoff sauce mix.*
- *Sliced sausage, spinach noodles, sour cream sauce mix, romano cheese.*
- *Dried chicken or chicken-style TVP (textured vegetable protein), instant rice, cream-of-chicken soup mix, dried onion flakes, and sunflower seeds.*
- *Canned chunk ham, dried potato slices, home-dried peas, cheese sauce mix from generic "au gratin" potatoes, dried milk, and Italian seasoning.*
- *Dried meat, instant mashed potatoes, dried milk, stuffing mix, gravy mix, and onion flakes.*
- *Bulgar, dried carrots, celery and onion, onion-soup mix, and cashews.*
- *Canned or dried shrimp, quick brown rice, home-dried green beans, and teriyaki sauce mix.*

To Dry Ground Beef

Brown lean ground beef thoroughly. Drain the fat. Rinse in a colander using hot water, and pat dry with paper towels. Dry meat on a cookie sheet in oven at lowest possible setting (prop door open about 1" with a wooden spoon). Dry 6 to 8 hours, until meat rsembles coarse gravel; it must be hard and dry.

Quantities

The packages will inform you, when shopping for ingredients, of how many servings each contains. Use this information to figure out how much to buy for the duration of the trip. Estimate 2 to 3 cups of cooked supper per person per meal, depending on their appetite. (See Chapter 2 for further discussion of quantities.)

Water

With one-pot meals, the amount of water required may vary. In deciding how much to use, notice how much water is called for. If separately the ingredients call for 2 cups water for the rice, for example, and 1 cup of water for the vegetables, and 1 cup for the textured vegetable protein, compromise at $3\frac{1}{2}$ cups to start with, and add more water later if it seems too thick or dry.

When to Add

Should you cook all the ingredients together or add some items at the end of the cooking time? Most dinners will cook in 15 minutes, so you might cook dried meats and dried vegetables along with dried soup, and add mashed potatoes, stuffing, or cream sauce at the end. Along with your salt supply, you might like to carry an extra container of garlic powder or onion powder or dried milk to add extra flavor to dinner.

Instructions

For one-pot meals, write notes and cooking instructions similar to those in this chapter. Enclose the instructions in your packages.

Easy Granola

MAKES NINE TO TEN CUPS

This can be stored in airtight containers at room temperature. Use within four weeks.

Preheat oven to 300 degrees.

In a large bowl, mix:

> **4 cups uncooked oatmeal (not instant)**
>
> **1 cup wheat germ**
>
> **$^1/_3$ cup dried milk**
>
> **1 cup flaked coconut**
>
> **$^1/_2$ cup sesame seeds**
>
> **1 cup sunflower seeds**
>
> **$^1/_2$ teaspoon salt**
>
> **1 cup blanched, slivered almonds**

In a small saucepan, heat until warm and sugar is dissolved:

> **$^1/_4$ cup oil**
>
> **$^1/_2$ cup honey**
>
> **$^1/_2$ cup brown sugar, packed**

Add, after mixture is warm and sugar is dissolved:

> **$1^1/_2$ teaspoons vanilla**

Pour oil mixture over oat mixture, stirring to mix well. Pour into a shallow 9" x 13" baking pan. Bake 25 to 30 minutes until golden brown, stirring every 10 minutes. During last 5 minutes of baking, stir in

$1^1/_2$ cups dried chopped fruit, if desired

Cool and store in airtight containers.

Campsite cooking instructions

Serve cold with water and powdered milk, or add hot water for a hot breakfast, or eat dry as a snack.

1 *Include campsite preparation instructions for those instructions in your package. See tear-out #1 in the pages in the back of this cookbook.*

GORP (Good Old Raisins and Peanuts)

Gorp is a hiking favorite because it keeps well and provides a lot of energy and calories. But, even a favorite can get boring, so variations of this snack mix have developed. I sent Alan and Dan a variety of gorp mixes to keep things interesting. The following variations are referred to by number on the menu lists:

Mix:

Gorp #1　　**1 part raisins**
　　　　　　1 part peanuts

Gorp #2　　**1 part banana chips**
　　　　　　1 part peanuts
　　　　　　1 part carob chips

Gorp #3　　**1 part chopped dates**
　　　　　　1 part walnuts
　　　　　　1 part coconut

Gorp #4　　**1 part mixed nuts**
　　　　　　1 part banana chips
　　　　　　1 part chopped dates

Gorp #5　　**1 part plain M & M's**
　　　　　　1 part cashews
　　　　　　1 part coconut

Gorp #6　　**1 part pretzel sticks**
　　　　　　1 part peanuts
　　　　　　1 part butterscotch chips

Gorp #7　　**1 part salted soy nuts**
　　　　　　1 part raisins

Gorp #8　　**1 part butterscotch chips**
　　　　　　1 part walnuts

Trail Mix

This is another variation of a trail-snack mix that was popular with the hikers. Every hiker has his or her favorite combinations of snacks and spreads. Use the gorp recipes to give yourself additional ideas.

Mix the following:

Pumpkin seeds

White chocolate chips

Carob chips

Raisins

Peanuts

Sunflower seeds

Honey/Butter/Peanut Butter

This was a favorite spread on crackers and appeared frequently on our menus.

At-home (prepackaging) preparation
In a bowl, blend the following ingredients well:

1 part honey

1 part margarine

1 part peanut butter

Prehike packaging instructions
Package in plastic containers—squeeze tubes tend to leak or malfunction.

Spotted Applesauce

SERVES TWO

Prehike packaging instructions

Package 1

1 cup chopped dried apples
1 cup brown sugar
1/4 cup raisins
1/2 teaspoon cinnamon
1/4 teaspoon nutmeg

Package 2

1/4 cup chopped roasted peanuts

Camp ingredients

Enough water to cover

Campsite cooking instructions

Add water to Package 1 ingredients to cover. Bring water to boil, then simmer until tender (about 5 minutes). Top with nuts (Package 2). Can soak ingredients overnight in water to cover.

2 *Include a copy of those instructions in your package. See tear-out #2 in the pages in the back of this cookbook.*

Ralston Cereal

SERVES TWO

SERVES TWO

Prehike packaging instructions

Package 1

    $1/2$ **teaspoon salt**

    1 cup Ralston wheat cereal

Package 2

    $2/3$ **cup dried milk**

Package 3

    $1/4$ **cup nuts**

Package 4

    $1/2$ **cup raisins**

Camp ingredients

    $2^1/4$ **cups water**

Campsite cooking instructions

Heat $2^1/4$ cups water to boiling. Stir in Package 1 (Ralston and salt), and return to boil. Remove pan from heat. Cover and let stand until cereal thickens. Add Packages 2, 3, and 4 (milk, nuts, and raisins).

3 *Include a copy of those instructions in your package. See tear-out #3 in the pages in the back of this cookbook.*

Scrambled Eggs

Prehike packaging instructions
Package all together:

> $1/2$ **cup dried egg powder**
> **2 tablespoons dried milk**
> **2 tablespoons bacon bits**
> $1/2$ **tablespoon dried onion**
> $1/2$ **tablespoon chopped, dried green pepper**

Camp ingredients

> **Squeeze Parkay or other bottled margarine**
> $1/3$ **cup water**

Campsite cooking instructions
Blend with $1/3$ cup water. Let set 10 minutes. Beat with fork.
Cook in skillet in which 1 tablespoon margarine has been melted.

4 *Include a copy of those instructions in your package.*
See tear-out #4 in the pages in the back of this cookbook.

Sunrise Spuds

Prehike packaging instructions
Package 1

> **1 cup potato flakes or instant potatoes**
> $1/2$ **cup dry milk**
> **2 teaspoons Butter Buds**
> scant $1/2$ **teaspoon salt**

Package 2

> **2 tablespoons bacon bits**

Camp ingredients

> **1 cup water**

Campsite cooking instructions
Boil 1 cup water. Put all ingredients in bowl and pour in boiling
water. Fluff with fork, and serve.

5 *Include a copy of those instructions in your package.*
See tear-out #5 in the pages in the back of this cookbook.

Wheat Cereal

Prehike packaging instructions

Package together:

1 cup finely cracked wheat or bulgar

$1/4$ cup dry milk

$1/2$ teaspoon salt

handful of raisins or dates

handful of walnuts

Camp ingredients

2 tablespoons Squeeze Parkay or other bottled margarine

4 cups water

Campsite cooking instructions

Boil 4 cups water. Stir in package. Add 2 tablespoons margarine, return to boil. Cover pot, remove from heat, and let stand 5-10 minutes.

6 *Include a copy of those instructions in your package. See tear-out #6 in the pages in the back of this cookbook.*

Muesli

Make a large quantity in advance, and store individually packaged bags (two servings per bag) in freezer until shipped.
Prehike packaging instructions

Package together in five airtight bags or containers:
>   2^1/$_2$ **cups rolled oats**
> ^{1}/$_2$ **cup wheat germ**
> ^{1}/$_4$ **cup bran**
> ^{1}/$_4$ **cup sunflower seeds**
> ^{1}/$_4$ **cup chopped walnuts**
> ^{1}/$_4$ **cup raisins**
> ^{1}/$_4$ **cup dried figs or dates**

Camp ingredients
>   **water (optional)**

Campsite cooking instructions

Add water to package ingredients to eat as breakfast cereal, or as dry snack.

 Include a copy of those instructions in your package. See tear-out #7 in the pages in the back of this cookbook.

Cream of Wheat

SERVES TWO

The hikers used this recipe when they wanted a cooked *breakfast, instead of instant Cream of Wheat,
which is what they liked when mixed cold with strawberry-flavored Carnation Instant Breakfast.*

Prehike packaging instructions

Package 1

> $1/4$ **teaspoon salt**
> $1/2$ **cup Cream of Wheat**

Package 2

> **2 heaping tablespoons dried milk**
> **2 tablespoons wheat germ**
> **2 tablespoons chopped walnuts**

Camp ingredients

> $2^{1}/4$ **cups water**

Campsite cooking instructions

Heat $2^{1}/4$ cups water to boiling. Add Package 1 slowly,
stirring constantly. Cook $2^{1}/2$ minutes or until thickened.
Stir in Package 2.

8 *Include a copy of those instructions in your package.
See tear-out #8 in the pages in the back of this cookbook.*

Instant Oatmeal

MULTIPLE SERVINGS

Start with quick oatmeal (cheapest when bought in bulk). If you are making large batches, mix one-third cup of dry milk for each cup of dried oatmeal, and add a touch of spice, such as ground cinnamon or nutmeg, sweetening to taste with white or brown sugar. A handful of toasted wheat germ, wheat bran, sesame seeds, or chopped nuts will add flavor and nutrition. Cooking isn't really necessary, since a few minutes in hot water softens everything nicely. Add dried fruits, if desired.

At-home (prepackaging) preparation

In a large bowl, mix together:

$1/3$ cup quick oatmeal

> **Cinnamon or nutmeg (to taste)**
> **White or brown sugar (to taste)**
> **Toasted wheat germ (optional)**
> **Sesame seeds (optional)**
> **Chopped nuts (optional)**

In blender or coffee mill, whir $1/3$ of the mix until powdered; this will become the thick "glue" that holds the rest together. Add back to mix.

Prehike packaging instructions

Package 1

Combine all ingredients.

Camp ingredients

> **water**

Campsite cooking instructions

Add boiling water to the mix in cup or container. Stir and enjoy.

9 *Include a copy of those instructions in your package. See tear-out #9 in the pages in the back of this cookbook.*

Choco-Camp Bread

MAKES ONE LOAF

The glazed candied fruit in this recipe is mostly a holiday item. Small stores have it only at that time of year.

At-home (prepackaging) preparation

In a mixing bowl, cream together:

2 sticks margarine

³/₄ cup brown sugar, packed

Add, one at a time (beating well after each):

6 eggs

Add:

1 tablespoon lemon juice

¹/₄ cup and 2 tablespoons sunflower seeds

In a separate bowl, mix:

1¹/₂ cup and 2 tablespoons whole wheat flour

¹/₄ cup soy flour

3 tablespoons dried milk

1 teaspoon baking powder

Add to dry ingredients, coating each piece:

1 cup glazed candied fruit

Slowly combine dry and wet mixtures.

Stir in:

1 cup semisweet chocolate chips

Put batter in a greased 9" x 5" pan. Bake 40 minutes in a preheated 325-degree oven. Cool bread 15 minutes before removing from pan.

Prehike packaging instructions

Let cool completely before sealing in plastic bag.

Health Bread

MAKES ONE LOAF

This bread is especially good spread with peanut butter.

At-home (prepackaging) preparation

In a mixing bowl, mix together:

> $1/2$ **cup honey**
>
> **1 egg**
>
> **1/2 cup plain yogurt**
>
> **1/2 cup milk**

Blend in:

> **1 cup oatmeal**
>
> **1 cup whole wheat flour**
>
> **1 cup All-Bran**
>
> $1^1/2$ **teaspoons baking powder**
>
> **1 teaspoon salt**

Pour into greased loaf pan. Bake at 325 degrees, approximately 45 minutes to 1 hour. Cool 10 minutes before removing from pan. Then, turn onto a cooling rack, and cover with a damp towel.

Prehike packaging instructions

Seal in plastic bags.

Honey Bread

MAKES TWO LOAVES

This bread keeps especially well.

At-home (prepackaging) preparation:

In a large bowl, cream thoroughly:

> **1 cup margarine**
> **$^1/_2$ cup brown sugar**

Stir in, individually:

> **$^1/_3$ cup light molasses**
> **2 tablespoons honey**
> **1 tablespoon sherry**
> **$^1/_2$ cup cold mashed potatoes (instant)**
> **$1^1/_4$ cups sunflower seeds**

In another bowl, combine:

> **$2^3/_4$ cups whole wheat flour**
> **$^1/_2$ cup (rounded) sifted soy flour**
> **$^1/_2$ cup (rounded) sesame seed meal (ground seeds)**
> **$^2/_3$ cup dried milk**

> **1 teaspoon anise seed**
> **$1^1/_2$ teaspoons cinnamon**
> **$^1/_4$ teaspoon baking soda**
> **pinch black pepper**
> **$^1/_2$ cup dried currants**

Fold dry mixture into wet, a little at a time. Add 1 tablespoon water if needed for moist batter. Mold dough with hands, and place in two, greased 9" x 5" pans. Bake $1^1/_4$ hours at 200 degrees or until done. Do not overbake. Cool 15 minutes before removing from pans.

Prehike packaging instructions

Seal in plastic bags.

Logan Bread

This bread keeps well.

At-home (prepackaging) preparation:
In a large bowl, beat together:

6 eggs
1 cup oil
1^1/$_2$ cups brown sugar
2 cups melted butter

Add:

1 cup honey
^{1}/$_2$ cup molasses

Stir in:

3 cups sifted white flour
3 cups sifted whole wheat flour
3 teaspoons baking powder
2 teaspoons salt

Add:

^{1}/$_2$ cup dried milk
1 cup wheat germ
2^1/$_2$ cups oatmeal
1^1/$_4$ cups nuts
2 cups raisins

Stir well. Pour into four 9" x 9" greased pans, and bake at 300 degrees for 35 minutes, or until done. Cut into squares.

Prehike packaging instructions
Seal in plastic bags.

Date-Nut Bread

At-home (prepackaging) preparation

Preheat oven to 325 degrees. Grease a regular-sized loaf pan or three mini-loaf pans. In a mixing bowl, add:

1 cup dates, cut up

Pour over dates:

1 cup boiling water

Add:

1 teaspoon baking soda

Let cool. Add:

1 tablespoon butter

1 cup sugar

1 egg

1 teaspoon vanilla

1½ cups flour

1 cup chopped nuts

Pour into loaf pan. Bake for 1¼ hours or until done. Remove from pan, and cool on a rack.

Prehike packaging instructions

Seal in plastic bags.

Pumpkin Bread

MAKES TWO REGULAR LOAVES OR FOUR SMALL LOAVES
Especially good when pecans are used.

At-home (prepackaging) preparation

Grease and flour 2 regular loaf or 4 mini-loaf pans. Preheat oven to 350 degrees. In a mixing bowl, cream:

> $2^3/_4$ **cups sugar**
>
> $2/_3$ **cup margarine**
>
> **Add, then mix together:**
>
> **4 eggs**
>
> **2 cups pumpkin (1 small can)**
>
> $2/_3$ **cup water**

Sift together, then add to first mixture:

> $3^1/_3$ **cups flour**
>
> $1^1/_2$ **teaspoons baking powder**
>
> $1^1/_2$ **teaspoons salt**
>
> **2 teaspoons baking soda**
>
> **1 teaspoon cinnamon**
>
> $1/_2$ **teaspoon nutmeg**

If desired, add:

> $2/_3$ **cup nuts (pecans especially), raisins, or dates**

Pour into loaf pans. Bake in 350-degree oven for 1 hour.

Prehike packaging instructions

Seal in plastic bags.

Aunt Emma's Zucchini Bread

MAKES TWO LOAVES OR FIVE MINI-LOAVES

At-home (prepackaging) preparation
Preheat oven to 350 degrees. Grease 2 loaf pans (or 5 mini-loaf pans). In a large bowl, mix together:

> **1 cup oil**
> **2 cups sugar**
> **3 eggs**

Sift together:

> **3 cups flour**
> **3 teaspoons cinnamon**
> **1 teaspoon baking soda**
> **$1/2$ teaspoon baking powder**
> **$1/2$ teaspoon salt**

Add:

> **2 teaspoons vanilla**
> **$1/2$ cup nuts (optional)**
> **2 cups grated zucchini**

Pour into loaf pans. Bake 350 degrees for 1 hour. Remove from pan, and cool on a rack.

Prehike packaging instructions
Seal in plastic bags.

Poppy-Seed Bread

MAKES TWO LOAVES

This was listed as an excellent snack for long-distance runners.

At-home (prepackaging) preparation
Grease 2 loaf pans, and preheat oven to 350 degrees. In a large bowl, mix together:

    1 box (18$\frac{1}{4}$ oz.) yellow-cake mix

    1 package (3$\frac{3}{8}$ oz.) coconut-cream pudding

    4 eggs

    $\frac{1}{8}$ cup poppy seeds

    1 cup hot water

    $\frac{1}{2}$ cup oil

Pour into loaf pans; bake at 350 degrees for 40 to 50 minutes (check after 40 minutes). Remove from pan, and cool on a rack.

Prehike packaging instructions
Seal in plastic bags.

Corn Crackers

MAKES TWO DOZEN

At-home (prepackaging) preparation
Preheat oven to 350 degrees. In a mixing bowl, combine:

    2 cups whole wheat flour

    1 cup cornmeal

    $\frac{1}{2}$ cup sesame seeds

    $\frac{1}{8}$ teaspoon salt

In another bowl, combine:

    $\frac{1}{4}$ cup oil

    2 tablespoons honey

    1 cup water (approximately)

Add the wet ingredients to the dry ingredients. Mix well with your hands, adding extra water if necessary. On a floured surface, roll the dough about $\frac{1}{4}$-inch thick. Cut into squares. Bake on an oiled cookie sheet at 350 degrees for 20 minutes or until crisp and lightly browned.

Prehike packaging instructions
Seal in plastic bags.

Carrot Cake

MAKES TWO LOAF-SIZED CAKES OR FOUR SMALL ONES

This carrot cake lasts for three weeks before spoiling.

At-home (prepackaging) preparation

Preheat oven to 325 degrees. Combine, creaming well:

> **1$^{1}/_{2}$ cups brown sugar, packed**
>
> **$^{3}/_{4}$ cup margarine**

Fold in (individually):

> **4 eggs, beaten**
>
> **1$^{1}/_{2}$ cups grated carrots**
>
> **1$^{1}/_{4}$ cups sunflower seeds**

In a bowl, mix:

> **1$^{1}/_{2}$ cups plus 2 tablespoons wheat flour, sifted**
>
> **$^{1}/_{4}$ cup soy flour, sifted**
>
> **$^{1}/_{3}$ cup ground sesame meal (grind sesame seeds in blender)**
>
> **$^{1}/_{3}$ cup dried milk**

> **1 teaspoon cinnamon**
>
> **1 teaspoon mace**
>
> **1 tablespoon baking powder**
>
> **$^{1}/_{2}$ teaspoon salt**

Stir dry ingredients slowly into wet ingredients. Pour batter into 2 regular loaf pans or 4 small ones. Bake for 35 minutes at 325 degrees. Cool cake 15 minutes before removing from pan. Let cake reach room temperature before wrapping it in bags.

Prehike packaging instructions

Seal in plastic bags.

Buckwheat Bread

Yeast breads such as this hold up best in cool or cold weather. You can make your own buckwheat flour by grinding buckwheat groats in the blender. Groats (whole grain kernels or those coarsely cracked) are found in natural-food stores.

At-home (prepackaging) preparation

In a large bowl, measure:

1 cup medium buckwheat groats (kasha)

Pour over the groats:

1¹⁄₄ cups boiling water

Let set for 20 minutes. In a measuring cup, add:

1 packet yeast
³⁄₄ cup warm water

When the yeast is dissolved and the buckwheat mixture is lukewarm, combine them in the bowl with:

1 tablespoon brown sugar
1 cup plain yogurt
1 tablespoon salt
¹⁄₄ cup oil

Mix in:

1 cup buckwheat or whole wheat flour
4¹⁄₂ to 5 cups white flour

Knead the dough until smooth and elastic (about 10 minutes). Put the dough in a greased bowl, turn, cover with a damp cloth, and let rise until double its size. Punch it down, shape into 2 large loaves or 4 small ones. Let rise in greased loaf pans until nearly double in size. Bake at 375 degrees 30 to 35 minutes or until done.

Prehike packaging instructions

Seal in plastic bags.

Seven-Grain Bread

Like other yeast breads, this holds up best in cool or cold weather.

At-home (prepackaging) preparation

In a large bowl, measure:

1 cup seven-grain cereal (available in natural-foods stores)

Pour over it:
1¹/₂ cups boiling water

Cool to lukewarm. In a cup, combine:
1 packet dried yeast
¹/₂ cup warm water

Add the dissolved yeast to the cooled cereal, along with:
¹/₂ cup honey
¹/₃ cup oil
2 teaspoons salt
2 eggs
3 cups whole wheat flour

Mix well. Work in:
2¹/₂ to 3 cups white flour

Knead 5 minutes, adding more flour if the dough is too sticky. Place the dough in a greased bowl, turning to coat its surfaces. Cover with a damp towel, and let rise in a warm place until double in volume. Punch the dough down, shape into 4 mini-loaves and let rise until nearly double in oiled aluminum mini-loaf pans (or 2 8-inch loaf pans). Bake at 375 degrees 40-45 minutes, and cool loaves on racks.

Prehike packaging instructions

Seal in plastic bags.

Swedish Limpa Bread

MAKES FOUR ROUND LOAVES

This yeast bread also holds up best in cool or cold weather.

At-home (prepackaging) preparation

Combine in a large bowl:

> **2 packets dry yeast**
> **1/2 cup warm water**

In a saucepan, scald:

> **1 1/2 cups milk**

Add:

> **2 tablespoons margarine**

Stir until margarine is melted. Let the mixture cool until lukewarm. Add it to the dissolved yeast, along with:

> **2 teaspoons caraway seeds**
> **1/2 teaspoon fennel seeds**
> **1/2 cup brown sugar, packed**
> **2 tablespoons molasses (light)**
> **grated peel from 1 orange**
> **2 1/2 cups rye flour**

Add, and mix thoroughly:

> **4 cups white flour**

Knead it for 10 minutes, then put it into a greased bowl, turning to coat its surfaces. Cover it with a damp towel, and let it rise until double. Punch the dough down, divide it into 4 parts, and let it stand for 10 minutes. Form into 4 round loaves. Put these on greased cookie sheets, and let them rise until double in size. Bake at 375 degrees for 30 minutes, and cool on racks.

Prehike packaging instructions

Seal in plastic bags.

Congo Bars

MAKES THIRTY-SIX BARS

A variation on this recipe is to use dark-brown sugar and butterscotch chips.

At-home (prepackaging) preparation:
In a saucepan, melt:

3 sticks margarine

Add:

1 lb. light brown sugar

3 eggs (one at a time, beating well after each)

Add, and mix well:

1 teaspoon vanilla

$^1/_2$ teaspoon salt

2 teaspoons baking powder

$2^2/_3$ cups flour

Add:

1 cup chocolate chips

1 cup chopped nuts

Spread in 12" x 17" greased pan, and bake in 350-degree oven for 20 minutes or until light brown. Cut into bars when cool.

Prehike packaging instructions
Seal in plastic bags.

Joe Frogger Cookies

MAKES TWO-AND-A-HALF DOZEN

These giant molasses cookies worked for both snacks and desserts.

At-home (prepackaging) preparation:

In a mixing bowl, sift together:

- **8 cups flour, sifted**
- **1 tablespoon salt**
- **1 teaspoon ginger**
- **1 teaspoon cloves**
- **1 teaspoon nutmeg**
- **1/2 teaspoon allspice**

In a small bowl, combine:

- **3/4 cup water**
- **1 tablespoon rum flavoring**

In another bowl, combine

- **2 teaspoons soda**
- **2 cups dark molasses**

In a large bowl, cream together:

- **1 cup shortening**
- **2 cups sugar**

Add half of the dry ingredients to the sugar and shortening, then half of the water and rum-flavoring mix. Then, add half of the molasses, blending well after each addition. Repeat. Chill dough overnight or for several hours. On well-floured surface, roll dough 1/4" thick and cut with 4-inch cutter. Bake at 375 degrees for 10-12 minutes on greased cookie sheet until lightly browned. Let stand a few minutes, then remove.

Prehike packaging instructions

Seal in plastic bags.

Gorp Squares

At-home (prepackaging) preparation:
In a mixing bowl, cream together:

$1/2$ **cup butter**
$1/2$ **cup brown sugar, packed**
Beat in:
$1/4$ **cup wheat germ**
$1/2$ **cup quick-cooking oats**
$1/2$ **cup whole wheat flour**
$1/2$ **cup all-purpose flour**
2 teaspoons grated orange rind

Pat into 8-inch square pan.

In another bowl, mix:

2 eggs
$1/4$ **cup brown sugar, packed**
1 cup almonds (whole)
$1/4$ **cup raisins**
$1/4$ **cup coconut**
$1/2$-**cup chocolate chips**

Pour over base, and spread out evenly. Bake at 350 degrees for 35 minutes. Cool and cut into 12 squares.

Prehike packaging instructions
Wrap individually in plastic wrap.

Hiker's Bars

At-home (prepackaging) preparation
In a large bowl, combine:

    1 (1-lb.) box powdered sugar (3^1/$_2$ cups)
    12 tablespoons melted butter
    2 cups (18 oz.) peanut butter
    3 cups Rice Krispies

Melt together:

    8 oz. (1^1/$_4$ cups) milk chocolate chips
    8 oz. semisweet chocolate chips

Pat peanut-butter mixture into lightly buttered 11" x 17" pan. Spread melted chocolate on top. Cool in refrigerator, and cut into bars later.

Prehike packaging instructions
Seal in plastic bags.

Mountain Bars

At-home (prepackaging) preparation
Melt in a double boiler:

    12 oz. butterscotch chips

Blend in:

    ^{1}/$_2$ cup honey

Add, and stir quickly to blend:

    ^{1}/$_2$ cup chopped nuts
    ^{1}/$_2$ cup toasted wheat germ
    ^{1}/$_2$ cup raisins
    ^{1}/$_2$ cup coconut

Pat mixture into a greased 9-inch square pan. When partly cool, cut into 36 1^1/$_2$-inch bars. Store in refrigerator or freezer.

Prehike packaging instructions
Seal in plastic bags.

ANZACS

MAKES ONE DOZEN COOKIES

ANZAC stands for Australian-New Zealand Army Corps. This is an original Australian recipe from World War I, when Australian women baked these cookies to send to their men on the beaches of Gallipoli. They were still fresh after an eight-week boat trip.

At-home (prepackaging) preparation

Preheat oven to 350 degrees. In a large bowl, combine and mix well:

> **1 cup whole wheat flour**
> **1 cup coconut**
> **$1/2$ cup brown sugar**
> **1 cup rolled oats**

In a small saucepan, melt:

> **$1/2$ cup butter**

Add:

> **2 tablespoons water**
> **$1/2$ teaspoon baking soda**
> **1 tablespoon honey**

Add wet ingredients to dry ingredients, and mix well with your hands. Shape into cookies, and bake on an oiled cookie sheet at 350 degrees for about 20 minutes or until nice and brown. Cool on a rack.

Prehike packaging instructions

Seal in plastic bags.

Pecan Crisps

MAKES FIFTY BARS

These cookies stay fresh and crisp for days.

At-home (prepackaging) preparation

Cream until light:

1 cup soft margarine

1 cup light brown sugar, packed

Beat in:

1 teaspoon vanilla

1 egg yolk (reserve egg white)

Sift and mix well:

2 cups flour

$^1/_2$ teaspoon salt

1 teaspoon cinnamon

Press into greased 15" x 10" x 1" pan, and brush top with slightly beaten egg white. Sprinkle with, and gently press in:

$^3/_4$ cup chopped pecans

Bake at 350 degrees about 25 minutes. Cut into 50 bars while warm. Remove to rack at once.

Prehike packaging instructions

Seal in plastic bags.

Monster Cookies

MAKES TWENTY-SEVEN DOZEN COOKIES, DEPENDING ON SIZE

This is a monster recipe for a monster hike. One problem you may encounter is finding something big enough to serve as a mixing bowl. Start out with the biggest bowl of the electric mixer, which should accommodate everything up to the last bit of peanut butter. From there, transfer the process to a huge kettle used for jelly-making for the final additions. The cookies don't all have to be baked at once, because the dough will keep indefinitely if refrigerated in a covered plastic container. Or, store some in the freezer, letting it thaw enough to spoon out easily at baking time. I often halved the recipe.

At-home (prepackaging) preparation

Cream together:

1 lb. margarine
2 lbs. brown sugar
4 cups white sugar

Beat in (one at a time):

12 eggs

Stir in:

1 tablespoon vanilla
1 tablespoon light corn syrup

Add, mixing well:

8 teaspoons baking soda

Stir in, in sequence:

3 lbs. peanut butter
18 cups quick oats
2 cups chocolate chips
1 lb. M & Ms

Drop by teaspoonfuls on cookie sheet, and bake at 350 degrees for 10 to 12 minutes.

Prehike packaging instructions

Baked cookies can be sealed in plastic bags and frozen until needed.

Fudge Scotch Squares

MAKES TWELVE SQUARES

If these squares are not removed as soon as they're cool, it becomes very difficult to do so.

At-home (prepackaging) preparation

Preheat oven to 350 degrees.

In a bowl, mix:

> $1^1/_2$ **cups graham cracker crumbs**
>
> **1 can sweetened condensed milk**
>
> **1 cup semisweet chocolate chips**
>
> **1 cup butterscotch chips**
>
> **1 cup coarsely chopped walnuts**

Press mixture into a well-greased (or sprayed with Pam), 9-inch square pan. Bake at 350 degrees for 30-35 minutes. Cool 5 minutes, cut into squares, and remove from dish.

Prehike packaging instructions

Seal in plastic bags.

Peanut-Butter Balls

MAKES 60 BALLS

You may need more peanut butter for this recipe. Use force to get balls to stick together.

At-home (prepackaging) preparation:

Mix thoroughly:

> $2^1/_4$ **cups peanut butter**
>
> $3^1/_4$ **cups dried milk**
>
> **1 cup brown sugar**
>
> $1^1/_2$ **cups granola (bulk foods)**

Form into balls. Wrap balls individually in plastic wrap.

Prehike packaging instructions

Seal in plastic bags.

Yum Balls

At-home (prepackaging) preparation

Mix together:

$1/2$ **cup honey**

$1/4$ **cup cooking oil**

Add:

$1/2$ **cup sunflower seeds**

In another bowl, combine:

$1/2$ **cup sunflower meal (sunflower seeds finely ground)**

$3/4$ **cup sesame meal (sesame seeds finely ground)**

$1/2$ **cup instant dried milk**

$1/2$ **cup carob powder**

$1/2$ **cup coconut**

Mix well.

Slowly add dry ingredients to honey mixture. Divide batter into 10 parts. Shape into balls, and knead for 2 minutes. Wrap individually in plastic wrap.

Prehike packaging instructions

Seal in plastic bags.

Coconut Balls

At-home (prepackaging) preparation
Mix (until very light and fluffy):

1 cup soft margarine
$1/2$ cup granulated or powdered sugar

Add, and mix well:

$1/2$ teaspoon salt
2 teaspoons vanilla
2 cups sifted flour

Refrigerate until easy to handle. Preheat oven to 350 degrees. Prepare:

20 pecan halves
shredded coconut

For each ball, shape some chilled dough into a 1-inch ball around half a pecan. Roll in shredded coconut and place on ungreased cookie sheet. Bake 12 minutes or until light brown.

Prehike packaging instructions
Seal in plastic bags.

Sesame Balls

MAKES TEN BALLS

Sesame balls are a good-tasting, long-lasting candy. They pack extremely well and won't spoil over time.

At-home (prepackaging) preparation
Preheat oven to 300 degrees. In a bowl, combine:

$1/3$ cup dried milk
$1/2$ cup coconut
$1 1/2$ cups sesame meal (grind sesame seeds in blender)

Add:

$1/4$ cup honey

Mix well. Form into 2-inch balls, and knead with hands for several minutes. Flatten each ball out on cookie sheet, $1/2$ inch thick. Bake in a 300-degree, preheated oven for 20 minutes. Cool, and package.

Prehike packaging instructions
Seal in plastic bags.

Arroz Con Queso

SERVES THREE

Serve this with tortilla chips, which should be shipped in a firm plastic container to keep them from crumbling.

Prehike packaging instructions

Package 1

1¼ cups rice

3 packets Lipton tomato Cup-A-Soup

¼ teaspoon garlic powder

¼ cup dried onion

¼ cup dried green pepper

2 teaspoons basil

1 teaspoon oregano

1½ teaspoons salt

Package 2

1 cup grated cheese or ½ cup parmesan cheese

Package 3

Tortilla chips

Camp ingredients

2 tablespoons Squeeze Parkay or other bottled margarine

4 cups water

Campsite cooking instructions

Add Package 1 and 2 tablespoons margarine to 4 cups water. Bring to boil. Simmer covered 15 minutes (less if using instant rice). Serve on tortilla chips (Package 3). Sprinkle cheese (Package 2) on top.

10 *Include a copy of those instructions in your package. See tear-out #10 in the pages in the back of this cookbook.*

Beef Jerky

YIELDS ABOUT THIRTY JERKY STRIPS

The hikers liked jerky both plain, as a snack, or cooked in one-pot meals. During preparation, uniform slices will shorten the drying time. It's best to use a meat slicer or have a butcher slice it for you. If you decide to slice the meat without an electric slicer, partially freeze it first to make cutting easier. Cut across the grain for increased tenderness.

At-home (prepackaging) preparation

Slice into long strips (³/₁₆ to ¹/₄ inch thick):

2¹/₂ pounds flank steak, trimmed of fat

Arrange strips in shallow dish or pan.

In a cup, combine:

¹/₂ cup soy sauce
¹/₄–¹/₂ teaspoon garlic powder
Freshly ground pepper, to taste

Pour over beef strips, and marinate 2 or more hours. Arrange strips on a rack over a baking sheet (don't overlap). Bake at 150 to 175 degrees, for 10 to 12 hours, until leathery. Halfway through cooking time, sprinkle on

Hickory-smoked salt or liquid, to taste

Test jerky for dryness by cooling a piece. When cool, it should crack when bent, but not break. There should be no moist spots.

Prehike packaging instructions

Jerky can be stored in an airtight container for up to one month. Seal in plastic bags.

Beef Pureé

YIELDS THREE-QUARTERS OF A CUP OF CRUMBLED MEAT

This can be used with several dishes, including Stroganoff (page 110)

At-home (prepackaging) preparation

In a bowl, combine:

> **$1/4$ cup soy sauce**
> **$1/4$ pound trimmed raw beef, cut up**

Marinate fifteen minutes. In a pressure cooker, add beef and:

about $1 1/4$ cups water

Cook until tender. Pureé meat in blender with $1/4$ cup of liquid. Spray 11" x 17" pan with nonstick spray. Spread pureed meat evenly on pan. Dry in 150-degree oven 4 hours, stirring occasionally. It is done when crisp.

Prehike packaging instructions

Seal in plastic bag.

Camper's Lentil Stew

SERVES THREE

Prehike packaging instructions

Package 1

1 packet dried Lipton onion soup

1/3 cup rice

1 cup lentils

1/4 cup dried carrots

**1/2 cup dried potatoes (from generic
"au gratin" potato packet)**

2 tablespoons dried, sliced mushrooms

1/2 teaspoon onion salt

1/4 teaspoon thyme (powdered)

1/8 teaspoon pepper

Camp ingredients

4 cups water

Campsite cooking instructions

Mix all ingredients with 4 cups water. Bring to boil, and simmer, covered 20 minutes.

11 *Include a copy of those instructions in your package.
See tear-out #11 in the pages in the back of this cookbook.*

Chicken and Nut Stir Pot

SERVES TWO

Prehike packaging instructions

Package 1

1 oz. dried chicken (or 5-oz. can)

1 packet onion soup mix

1 packet chicken noodle soup mix

1 packet chicken gravy mix

1 cup rice

Package 2

¼ cup nuts (any kind)

Camp ingredients

3 cups water

Squeeze Parkay or other bottled margarine (generous portion)

Campsite cooking instructions

Add Package 1 to 3 cups water and margarine. Bring to boil. Lower heat and cook 15 minutes or until rice is tender, stirring frequently. Add nuts as desired.

12 *Include a copy of those instructions in your package. See tear-out #12 in the pages in the back of this cookbook.*

Chicken and Rice Curry

SERVES TWO

Prehike packaging instructions

1 cup long-grain rice

Package 2

1 package chicken-noodle soup

1 teaspoon curry

Package 3

1 oz. dried chicken (or 5-oz. can)

Package 4

¹/₂ cup raisins

Camp ingredients

**1 tablespoon Squeeze Parkay
or other bottled margarine**

3¹/₄ cups water

Campsite cooking instructions

Combine all with 1 tablespoon margarine and 3¹/₄ cups water, and bring to boil. Simmer 15 minutes (covered), stirring occasionally.

13 *Include a copy of those instructions in your package.
See tear-out #13 in the pages in the back of this cookbook.*

Chicken Klister with Peas

The peas should be home-dried or freeze-dried; don't buy supermarket split peas—they take hours to cook.

Prehike packaging instructions

Package 1

> **4 oz. macaroni**
>
> **1 oz. dried chicken (or 5-oz. can)**
>
> **1 tablespoon chicken bouillon granules (can crush cubes into granules)**
>
> **1 tablespoon onion soup mix**
>
> **$1/4$ cup home-dried peas**
>
> **$1/2$ teaspoon dill weed**

Package 2

> **1 packet sour cream mix**

Package 3

> **$1/4$ cup slivered almonds**

Camp ingredients

> **$3^{1}/_{2}$ cups water**

Campsite cooking instructions

Bring $3^{1}/_{2}$ cups water and Package 1 to boil. Simmer 15 minutes. Meanwhile, add $1/2$ cup cold water to sour cream, and beat with fork for 1 minute. Stir in almonds and sour cream just before serving.

14 *Include a copy of those instructions in your package. See tear-out #14 in the pages in the back of this cookbook.*

Chicken Rag-Out

SERVES TWO

One-pot meal. If you are a solo hiker carrying only one cooking pot, you might use tortilla chips or pretzel sticks as an accompaniment.

Prehike packaging instructions
Package 1

$^1/_2$ cup dried sliced carrots

$^1/_4$ cup dried sliced celery

$^1/_4$ cup dried potato (from generic "au gratin" packet)

2 tablespoons dried sliced mushrooms

2 tablespoons dried chopped onion

2 teaspoons dried parsley flakes

$^1/_2$ cup home-dried peas

2 cubes chicken bouillon

1 oz. dried chicken (or 5-oz. can boneless chicken)

pinch of anise seed

pepper to taste

Package 2

1 packet Lipton Noodles & Sauce (sour cream and chives flavor)

Camp ingredients

3 cups water for Chicken Rag-Out, additional water for Lipton noodles

Squeeze Parkay or other bottled margarine (for Lipton noodles)

Additional water as required.

Campsite cooking instructions
Simmer all ingredients in 3 cups water for 15 minutes. Add more water if necessary.

15 *Include a copy of those instructions in your package.*
See tear-out #15 in the pages in the back of this cookbook.

Chicken Stew

Prehike Packaging Instructions

Package 1

    2 packets Lipton Cream-O-Chicken Cup-A-Soup

    $1/2$ cup dried green beans

    1 oz. dried chicken (or 5-oz. can)

Package 2

    1 cup potato flakes

    scant $1/2$ teaspoon salt

    $1/2$ cup dried milk

Camp Ingredients

    $3^1/2$ cups water

    **$1^1/2$ tablespoon Squeeze Parkay
or other bottled margarine**

Campsite cooking instructions

Bring Package 1 and $1^1/2$ tablespoon margarine boil in $3^1/2$ cups water. Simmer 15 minutes. Stir in Package 2 until just moistened. Let rest 1 minute, and fluff with fork.

16 *Include a copy of those instructions in your package.
See tear-out #16 in the pages in the back of this cookbook.*

Chili-To-Go

This recipe requires two pots on the Trail, if served with noodles.

At-home (prepackaging) preparation

In a skillet, brown:

> **1 pound ground chuck**

Spoon fat off. Add:

> **$1/2$ cup onion, finely chopped**
> **2 cloves minced garlic**
> **$1/3$ cup finely chopped green pepper**
> **$1/4$ teaspoon oregano**
> **$1/8$ teaspoon powdered cumin**
> **1 tablespoon chili powder**
> **$1/2$ teaspoon salt**
> **6-oz. can tomato paste**

Cook, stirring, for 15 minutes. Let sit one hour to enhance the flavor. Spread the chili on a greased shallow pan, and dry in oven. Set the oven temperature at its lowest setting (just barely on), and leave oven door open a crack. Let dry overnight (6-8 hours).

Prehike packaging instructions

Package 1

> **1 bag of dried chili mix**

Package 2

> **1 packet Lipton Noodles & Sauce (alfredo flavor)**

Camp ingredients

> **2 cups water for chili, additional water for Lipton noodles.**

Campsite cooking instructions

Add 2 cups water to the 2 cups dried chili. Stir and bring to boil. Cover and cook slowly 10 minutes. Prepare Lipton Noodles & Sauce (Package 2) according to packet directions.

17 *Include a copy of those instructions in your package. See tear-out #17 in the pages in the back of this cookbook.*

Chipped Beef and Broccoli Dish

SERVES TWO

*Since dried beef is generally found in five-ounce glass jars, and not always available in a sealed plastic bag
as it once was, you might want to either vacuum-pack the needed portions yourself or substitute another meat
(such as pepperoni or salami) that is already sealed in plastic and does not require refrigeration.*

Prehike packaging instructions

Package 1

1 packet Lipton Pasta & Sauce (cheddar-broccoli)

$1/3$ cup dried broccoli soup (found in bulk-foods section of grocery)

$2/3$ cup dried milk

$1/4$ cup elbow macaroni

Package 2

$1/2$ packet (5 oz.) chipped beef

Camp ingredients

3 cups water

2 tablespoons Squeeze Parkay or other bottled magarine

Campsite Cooking Instructions

Boil 3 cups water and 2 tablespoons margarine. Add Package 1 and cook 10 minutes, stirring as needed. Chop half the packet of chipped beef (Package 2), and add to Package 1 the last couple minutes of cooking time. (Save the other half for use another day.) Add more water if needed.

18 *Include a copy of those instructions in your package.
See tear-out #18 in the pages in the back of this cookbook.*

Chipped Beef and Creamed Peas

SERVES TWO

This recipe requires two pots for campsite preparation. (See dried-beef note on page 92.)

Prehike packaging instructions

Package 1

$^1/_2$ **packet (5 oz.) chipped beef (leave sealed in original packet)**

Package 2

$^3/_4$ cup home-dried peas

Package 3

1 packet white sauce

Package 4

1$^1/_2$ cups potato flakes
$^3/_4$ cup dried milk

Camp ingredients

4 cups water

2 tablespoons Squeeze Parkay or other bottled margarine

Campsite Cooking Instructions

In one pot, chop beef (Package 1) and add Package 2 (peas) and 2$^1/_2$ cups water. Bring to boil. Simmer 15 minutes. In small pot, stir together Package 3 (white sauce) and 1$^1/_2$ cup water. Boil, then simmer 1 minute, stirring constantly. Stir in Package 4 (potatoes) and white sauce.

19 *Include a copy of those instructions in your package. See tear-out #19 in the pages in the back of this cookbook.*

Chipped Beef Stew

SERVES TWO

See the note about the availability of dried beef on page 92.

Prehike packaging instructions

Package 1

> **1 packet Knorr mushroom soup**
>
> **1 cup dried potatoes (from generic "au gratin" potato packet)**
>
> **$1/4$ cup dried green beans**
>
> **$1/4$ cup dried carrot slices**
>
> **2 teaspoons dried onion**
>
> **2 teaspoons dried celery**

Package 2

> **$1/2$ packet (5 oz.) chipped beef**

Camp Ingredients

> **4 cups water**

Campsite Cooking Instructions

Cook Package 1 (soup and vegetables) in 3 to $3^1/2$ cups water for 15 minutes. Chop chipped beef (Package 2). Add extra $1/2$ cup water and chipped beef to the cooked soup mixture.

20 *Include a copy of those instructions in your package. See tear-out #20 in the pages in the back of this cookbook.*

Corn Chowder

Prehike packaging instructions

Package 1

- ²/₃ **cup dried corn**
- ¹/₄ **cup home-dried peas**
- 2 **tablespoon dried onion**
- ¹/₄ **teaspoon dry mustard**
- ¹/₂ **teaspoon salt**
- ¹/₈ **teaspoon pepper**

Package 2

- ¹/₂ **cup dried milk**
- 1 **cup mashed potato flakes**
- 2 **tablespoon bacon bits**

Camp ingredients

- **4 cups water**
- **2 tablespoons Squeeze Parkay or other bottled margarine**

Campsite cooking instructions

Add Package 1 (vegetables) to 4 cups water. Bring to boil, and simmer 15 minutes. Add Package 2 (milk and potatoes), and simmer a few more minutes. Add 2 tablespoons margarine.

 Include a copy of those instructions in your package. See tear-out #21 in the pages in the back of this cookbook.

Curried Vegetables

Prehike packaging instructions

Package 1

2 oz. packet vegetable soup

Package 2

1½ cups minute rice
1½ teaspoons curry powder

Package 3

½ cup raisins

Package 4

¼ cup nuts

Package 5

¼ cup coconut

Camp Ingredients

2¼ cups water

Campsite cooking instructions

Mix Package 1 (soup) with 2¼ cups water. Bring to a boil, stirring occasionally. Simmer 10 minutes. Remove from heat, and stir in Package 2 (rice). Let stand 5 minutes. Add raisins and nuts; sprinkle coconut on top.

22 *Include a copy of those instructions in your package. See tear-out #22 in the pages in the back of this cookbook.*

Deb's African Peanut Stew

Prehike packaging instructions

Package 1

   1 oz. dried chicken (or 5-oz. can)

   3 cubes chicken bouillon

   2 tablespoons dried onion

   ¹⁄₄ cup dried carrot slices

   ¹⁄₄ cup rice

   ¹⁄₂ teaspoon salt

   ¹⁄₈ teaspoon cayenne pepper

Package 2

   ¹⁄₂ cup peanut butter (in plastic container)

Camp Ingredients

   3 cups water

Campsite cooking instructions

Bring 3 cups water and Package 1 (chicken) to boil, and simmer 15 minutes. Stir in Package 2 (peanut butter).

23 *Include a copy of those instructions in your package. See tear-out #23 in the pages in the back of this cookbook.*

Expedition Spaghetti

SERVES TWO

Prehike packaging instructions

Package 1

    4 oz. spaghetti (broken)

Package 2

    4 oz. salami, or $1/2$ cup meatless-burger mix (textured vegetable protein or Gran Burger)

    $1/2$ packet spaghetti-sauce mix with mushrooms

Package 3

    4 packets Lipton Tomato Cup-a-Soup

Package 4

    $1/4$ cup parmesan cheese

Camp ingredients

    4 cups water

    Squeeze Parkay or other bottled margarine

Campsite cooking instructions

Bring $3^{1/2}$ cups water and Packages 1 and 2 (spaghetti and meat sauce) to boil. Cook ten minutes. Remove from heat. Stir in Package 3 (soup). Sprinkle cheese over all.

24 *Include a copy of th0se instructions in your package. See tear-out #24 in the pages in the back of this cookbook.*

Fontana Dinner

SERVES TWO

Prehike packaging instructions

Package 1

   ¹/₄ cup dried onion

   ¹/₄ cup dried carrots

   2 tablespoons dried parsley flakes

   ⁵/₈ cup quick brown rice

   1¹/₂ cubes beef bouillon

   pepper

Package 2

   4-oz. packet shredded cheddar cheese

Camp ingredients

   3 cups water

Campsite Cooking Instructions

Bring 3 cups water and Package 1 (rice and vegetables) to boil, and simmer until tender, 12-15 minutes. Top with Package 2 (shredded cheese). Serve when cheese has melted.

25 *Include a copy of those instructions in your package.*
See tear out #25 in the pages in the back of this cookbook.

Green Pea-Brown Rice Mix

Prehike packaging instructions

Package 1

1 box (5 oz.) brown & wild rice with mushrooms

1 envelope instant green pea soup

Combine rice and seasoning packet contents with soup powder in a plastic bag.

Package 2

¼ cup chopped nuts

Camp ingredients

2 cups water

**ample portion Squeeze Parkay
or other bottled margarine**

Campsite cooking instructions

Add 2 cups water and margarine to Package 1 (rice). Bring to boil. Lower heat, and simmer 20 minutes. Serve with nuts (Package 2).

26 *Include a copy of those instructions in your package. See tear-out #26 in the pages in the back of this cookbook.*

Hash Brown Potatoes

For hash browns, we simply used half a package of Betty Crocker hash brown potato mix, prepared according to the package instructions. If you'd rather mix your own, here's another recipe. It requires a pot and a skillet.

Prehike packaging instructions

Package 1

> **1 cup finely diced dried potatoes (from generic "au gratin" potato packet)**
>
> **$^1/_2$ tablespoon dried onion flakes**

Package 2

> **1 teaspoon parsley flakes**
>
> **$^1/_4$ teaspoon salt**
>
> **$^1/_8$ teaspoon pepper**

Camp Ingredients

> **water**
>
> **2 tablespoons Squeeze Parkay or other bottled margarine**

Campsite Cooking Instructions

In pan, cover Package 1 with boiling water. Let stand for 20 minutes. Drain. Stir in Package 2. In skillet, heat margarine. Spread potato mix evenly in hot skillet. Stir slowly until underside is golden brown. Turn, and brown other side.

27 *Include a copy of those instructions in your package. See tear out #27 in the pages in the back of this cookbook.*

101

Hawaiian Chicken

Prehike packaging instructions

Package 1

> **1 oz. dried chicken (or 5-oz. can)**
>
> **$^1/_4$ cup dried pineapple, chopped**
>
> **$^1/_4$ cup dried carrots**
>
> **1 tablespoon dried green pepper, minced**

Package 2

> **1 cup minute rice**
>
> **scant $^1/_2$ teaspoon salt**
>
> **1 packet Sweet-and-Sour Sauce mix**

Package 3

> **$^1/_4$ cup cashews or slivered almonds**

Camp ingredients

> **2 cups water**
>
> **1 tablespoon Squeeze Parkay or other bottled margarine**

Campsite cooking instructions

Bring 2 cups water, 1 tablespoon margarine, and Package 1 (chicken) to boil. Simmer 10 minutes. Stir in Package 2 (rice), and remove from heat. Add more water if necessary. Let stand 5 minutes. Add cashews (Package 3).

28 *Include a copy of those instructions in your package. See tear-out #28 in the pages in the back of this cookbook.*

Isle Royale Dinner

Prehike packaging instructions

Package together:

$^3/_4$ **cup dried milk**

$^3/_4$ **cup TVP (textured vegetable protein)**

$^3/_4$ **cup dried mixed vegetables**

$1^1/_2$ **boxes Rice-A-Roni**

$1^1/_2$ **Rice-A-Roni seasoning packets**

Camp Ingredients

$3^1/_2$ **cups water**

Campsite Cooking Instructions

Add package to $3^1/_2$ cups water, bring to boil, and simmer 15 minutes.

29 *Include a copy of those instructions in your package.*
See tear-out #29 in the pages in the back of this cookbook.

Kasha (Buckwheat Groats)

SERVES TWO

This recipe works with meat or as side dish. There's a difference between grits and groats—grits are finer.)

Prehike packaging instructions
Package 1

$1/2$ cup buckwheat groats
   $1/4$ teaspoon salt
   3 tablespoons dried milk
   1 tablespoon dried onion
   1 tablespoon dried green pepper

Camp Ingredients
   $1^1/4$ cups water
   1 tablespoons margarine

Campsite Cooking Instructions
Add ingredients to $1^1/4$ cup of water and 1 tablespoon of margarine. Bring to boil and simmer, covered, 15 minutes, stirring occasionally.

30 *Include a copy of those instructions in your package. See tear-out #30 in the pages in the back of this cookbook.*

Manhattan Clam Chowder

SERVES TWO

Prehike packaging instructions

Package 1

> $1/2$ cup dried potatoes (from generic "au gratin" potato packet)
>
> $1/2$ cup tomato flakes
>
> $1/4$ cup dried celery
>
> $1/4$ cup dried onion
>
> 2 teaspoons bacon bits
>
> $1/2$ teaspoon salt
>
> $1/8$ teaspoon pepper

Package 2

> $1/2$ cup dried milk
>
> $1/4$ cup instant mashed potatoes

Package 3

> $6^{1}/_{2}$-oz. can minced clams

Camp ingredients

> 3 cups water

Campsite Cooking Instructions

Cook Package 1 in 3 cups water for 10 minutes. Add Package 2 and undrained clams (Package 3). Cook 5 additional minutes. Add more water if needed.

31 *Include a copy of those instructions in your package.*
See tear out #31 in the pages in the back of this cookbook.

Mountain Chowder

Prehike packaging instructions

Package 1

- **¹/₂ cup (rounded) dried corn**
- **¹/₄ cup dried onion**
- **2 tablespoons dried celery**
- **1 tablespoon dried green pepper**
- **¹/₃ cup dried tomato flakes**
- **¹/₂ tablespoon parsley flakes**
- **¹/₂ teaspoon sugar**
- **¹/₄ teaspoon paprika**
- **¹/₄ teaspoon salt**
- **¹/₈ teaspoon pepper**

Package 2

- **¹/₂ cup potato flakes**
- **¹/₄ cup dried milk**
- **¹/₄ cup bacon bits**

Camp Ingredients

3 cups water

Campsite cooking instructions

Add Package 1 (vegetables) to 3 cups of water. Bring water to a boil, and simmer 15 minutes. Add Package 2 (potatoes), and simmer a few more minutes.

32 *Include a copy of those instructions in your package. See tear-out #32 in the pages in the back of this cookbook.*

Safari Surprise

Prehike packaging instructions

Package 1

¹/₂ cup dried shrimp (found in Oriental stores)

Package 2

¹/₂ cup lentils

Package 3

**1 packet lobster bisque mix
(or dried mushroom soup)**

2 teaspoons dried parsley

2 tablespoons dried celery

1 tablespoon dried green pepper

¹/₄ cup dried carrots

Package 4

1 cup instant rice

scant ¹/₂ teaspoon salt

Camp ingredients

3 cups water

Campsite Cooking Instructions

Mix Packages 1, 2, and 3 in 3 cups water. Bring to boil, and simmer 15 minutes. Stir in Package 4, and let stand 5 minutes.

33 *Include a copy of those instructions in your package. See tear-out #33 in the pages in the back of this cookbook.*

Shrimp-Rice Dinner

SERVES TWO

Prehike packaging instructions

Package 1

    1 packet "Golden Dipt" shrimp bisque or dried mushroom soup

    1 teaspoon parsley

    1½ cups minute rice

Package 2

    4½-oz. can shrimp or 2 oz. dried shrimp

Camp Ingredients

    2 cups water

    Squeeze Parkay or other bottled margarine

Campsite cooking instructions

Bring 2 cups of water to a boil. Stir in Package 1 (rice). (If using dried shrimp, add now.) Cover, and let sit for 10 minutes. Drain canned shrimp (Package 2). Add to rice mixture. Stir, and cover for 5 minutes. Add margarine if desired.

 Include a copy of those instructions in your package. See tear-out #34 in the pages in the back of this cookbook.

Spanish Rice

SERVES TWO

Prehike packaging instructions
Package 1

    1 box Rice-A-Roni

    $^1/_4$ cup dried tomatoes

    1 tablespoon dried, chopped green pepper

    $^1/_2$ cup dried mixed vegetables

    $^1/_2$ cup TVP (textured vegetable protein)

Camp Ingredients
    3 $^1/_4$ cups water

Campsite cooking instructions
Bring 3$^1/_4$ cups and all ingredients to boil in pot, and simmer 15 minutes.

35 **36** *Include a copy of those instructions in your package. See tear-outs #35 and #36 in the pages in the back of this cookbook.*

St. Patrick's Stew

SERVES TWO

Prehike packaging instructions
Package 1

    3 oz. uncooked spinach noodles

    $^3/_4$ cup instant rice

    1 packet (2 oz.) noodle soup with chicken broth

    1 tablespoon chicken bouillon granules

Package 2

    $^3/_4$ cup slivered almonds

Package 3

$^3/_4$ cup raisins

Camp ingredients
    4 cups water

Campsite cooking instructions
Boil 4 cups water and Package 1 (noodles); cook 8 minutes.
Add more water if needed. Stir in almonds and raisins, and serve.

Stroganoff

Packets of stroganoff mix and sour cream mix should be available at most supermarkets, in the dried-gravy section.
This recipe requires two pots.

Prehike packaging instructions

Package 1

$^2/_3$ cup dried milk

1 packet sour cream mix

1 packet stroganoff mix

Package 2

2 cups noodles

$^1/_2$ cup dried beef puree (see recipe, page 84)

$^1/_2$ teaspoon salt

2 tablespoons dried mushrooms

Camp Ingredients

$4^1/_2$ cups water

4 tablespoons margarine

Campsite cooking instructions

Mix $1^1/_2$ cups water to Package 1 (stroganoff mix) in small pot. Heat and simmer until sauce thickens. Cover, and remove from heat. Add Package 2 (beef and noodles) to 3 cups water in large pot. Bring to boil, and simmer 15 minutes. Stir in sauce. Add margarine.

37 *Include a copy of those instructions in your package. See tear-out #37 in the pages in the back of this cookbook.*

Turkey Trail Dinner

SERVES TWO

This "turkey" is actually chicken, with turkey stuffing and flavorings. When planning your menus, consider packaging two dinners at the same time, since the recipe calls for half-packages of several items.

Prehike packaging instructions

Package 1

$^1/_2$ **seasoning packet (in stuffing mix)**

1 oz. dried chicken (or 5-oz. can)

$^1/_2$ **packet turkey gravy mix**

1 teaspoon dried onion flakes

scant $^1/_2$ teaspoon salt

Package 2

$^1/_2$ **box turkey-flavored stuffing mix**

1$^1/_3$ cups dried potato flakes

2 tablespoons dried milk

Camp ingredients

2 tablespoons Squeeze Parkay or other bottled margarine

Campsite cooking instructions

Combine Package 1 (chicken) with 3 cups water and 2 tablespoons margarine. Bring to boil, and simmer 10 minutes. Remove from heat. Stir in Package 2 (stuffing). Cover, and let stand 5 minutes.

38 *Include a copy of those instructions in your package. See tear-out #38 in the pages in the back of this cookbook.*

Tuna Fettucini

This recipe requires two pots for campsite preparation.

Prehike packaging instructions

Package 1

    1 oz. dried tuna (or 6^1/$_2$-oz. can or pouch)

    3 oz. fettucini (broken)

    dash garlic powder

    1 tablespoon dried green pepper

    ^{1}/$_4$ cup dried celery

    ^{1}/$_8$ teaspoon salt

    dash pepper

Package 2

    1 packet white sauce

    ^{1}/$_2$ cup parmesan cheese

    ^{1}/$_2$ cup dried milk

Camp Ingredients

    4 cups water

Campsite cooking instructions

Bring 3 cups water and Package 1 to boil, and simmer
12 minutes. Add 1 cup water to Package 2 in small pan.
Stirring constantly, bring to boil, and simmer on low heat
1 minute. Stir into tuna mixture, and serve.

39 *Include a copy of those instructions in your package.
See tear-out #39 in the pages in the back of this cookbook.*

White Mountain Stew

SERVES TWO

Black-eyed peas require the full cooking time, or they will be hard and crunchy.

Prehike packaging instructions

Package 1

¹/₄ cups dried black-eyed peas

³/₄ cup dried mixed vegetables

1 teaspoon beef bouillon granules

¹/₂ teaspoon onion salt

Package 2

³/₄ cup couscous (quick cooking)

Camp ingredients

3¹/₂ cups water

**generous serving Squeeze Parkay
or other bottled margarine**

salt

Campsite Cooking Instructions

Bring 3¹/₂ cups water and Package 1 (vegetables) to boil, and simmer 15 minutes. Add couscous (Package 2), and simmer 5 additional minutes. Serve with generous helping of margarine and salt.

40 *Include a copy of those instructions in your package.
See tear-out #40 in the pages in the back of this cookbook.*

Appendix

A.T. Mileage Chart

This chart, current as of January 2009, will help you plan your mail drops during an Appalachian Trail thru-hike. It is adapted from the Appalachian Trail Conservancy's *Appalachian Trail Thru-Hike Planner,* which contains a series of checklists and resources for those planning a long-distance hike on the A.T. The number of miles per day that you cover will change during a thru-hike, and you will probably have to recalculate your plans as your hike progresses.

SOUTHBOUND Days from last point at 8 / 12 / 25 miles per day			Miles from Katahdin	DROP POINT	ZIP Code	Miles off A.T.	Miles from Springer	NORTHBOUND Days from last point at 8 / 12 / 25 miles per day		
				Katahdin Terminus			2,178.3	15	10	5
15	10	5	114.6	Monson, Maine	04464	4.0	2,063.7	5	3	2
5	3	2	151.3	Caratunk, Maine	04925	0.3	2,027.0	5	3	2
5	3	2	187.9	Stratton, Maine	04982	5.0	1,990.4	6	4	2
6	4	2	220.1	Rangeley, Maine	04970	9.0	1,958.2	5	4	2
5	4	2	246.5	Andover, Maine	04216	9.0	1,931.8	8	5	3
8	5	3	297.9	Gorham, N.H.	03581	3.6	1,880.4	3	2	1
3	2	2	319.0	Pinkham Notch Camp			1,859.3	7	5	2
7	5	3	372.7	North Woodstock, N.H.	03262	5.8	1,805.6	4	3	1

SOUTHBOUND Days from last point at 8 12 25 miles per day			Miles from Katahdin	DROP POINT	ZIP Code	Miles off A.T.	Miles from Springer	NORTHBOUND Days from last point at 8 12 25 miles per day		
4	3	1	398.5	Glencliff, N.H.	03238	0.4	1,779.8	1	1	0
1	1	0	403.4	Warren, N.H.	03279	4.0	1,774.9	2	1	1
2	1	1	408.2	Wentworth, N.H.	03282	4.3	1,770.1	5	3	2
5	3	2	441.8	Hanover, N.H.	03755		1,736.5	0	0	0
0	0	0	443.3	Norwich, Vt.	05055	0.3	1,735.0	1	1	0
1	1	0	451.6	West Hartford, Vt.	05084	0.3	1,726.7	2	1	0
2	1	0	462.7	South Pomfret, Vt.	05067	0.9	1,715.6	1	1	0
1	1	0	464.2	Woodstock, Vt.	05091	4.4	1,714.1	3	2	1
3	2	1	484.6	Killington, Vt.	05751	0.6	1,693.7	4	3	1
4	3	1	511.6	Wallingford, Vt.	05773	2.7	1,666.7	2	1	1
2	1	1	519.9	Danby, Vt.	05739	3.2	1,658.4	3	2	1
3	2	1	537.7	Manchester Center, Vt.	05255	5.8	1,640.6	6	4	2
6	4	2	577.8	Bennington, Vt.	05201	5.0	1,600.5	3	2	1
3	2	1	596.2	North Adams, Mass.	01247	2.5	1,582.1	1	1	0
1	1	0	602.5	Bascom Lodge, Mt. Greylock			1,575.8	1	1	0
1	1	0	610.8	Cheshire, Mass.	01225		1,567.5	1	1	0
1	1	0	619.5	Dalton, Mass.	01226		1,558.8	2	1	1

SOUTHBOUND Days from last point at 8 12 25 miles per day			Miles from Katahdin	DROP POINT	ZIP Code	Miles off A.T.	Miles from Springer	NORTHBOUND Days from last point at 8 12 25 miles per day		
2	1	1	629.1	Becket, Mass.	01223	5.0	1,549.2	2	2	1
2	2	1	638.5	Lee, Mass.	01238	5.0	1,539.8	2	1	1
2	1	1	648.2	Tyringham, Mass.	01264	0.6	1,530.1	3	2	1
3	2	1	667.6	Great Barrington, Mass.	01230	1.8	1,510.7	1	1	0
1	1	0		Sheffield, Mass.	01257	3.2		1	1	0
1	1	0	671.2	South Egremont, Mass.	01258	1.2	1,507.1	2	2	1
2	2	1	689.0	Salisbury, Conn.	06068	0.8	1,489.3	1	1	0
1	1	0	697.2	Falls Village, Conn.	06031	0.5	1,481.1	1	1	0
1	1	0	706.5	West Cornwall, Conn.	06796	2.2	1,471.8	1	1	0
1	1	0	711.3	Cornwall Bridge, Conn.	06754	0.9	1,467.0	2	1	1
2	1	1	722.4	Kent, Conn.	06757	0.8	1,455.9	2	1	1
2	1	1	733.9	Wingdale, N.Y.	12594	3.3	1,444.4	2	1	1
2	1	1	743.1	Pawling, N.Y.	12564	3.1	1,435.2	1	1	0
1	1	0	748.3	Poughquag, N.Y.	12570	3.1	1,430.0	2	1	0
2	1	0	755.5	Stormville, N.Y.	12582	1.9	1,422.8	4	3	1
4	3	1	780.0	Peekskill, N.Y.	10566	4.8	1,398.3	1	1	0
1	1	0	785.8	Ft. Montgomery, N.Y.	10922	0.7	1,392.5	3	2	1

SOUTHBOUND Days from last point at 8 12 25 miles per day			Miles from Katahdin	DROP POINT	ZIP Code	Miles off A.T.	Miles from Springer	NORTHBOUND Days from last point at 8 12 25 miles per day		
3	2	1	804.4	Arden, N.Y.	10910	0.7	1,373.9	2	1	1
2	1	1	816.4	Bellvale, N.Y.	10912	1.6	1,361.9	2	2	1
				Greenwood Lake, N.Y.	10925	2.0				
2	2	1	831.5	Vernon, N.J.	07462	2.4	1,346.8	1	0	0
1	0	0	833.8	Glenwood, N.J.	07418	1.1	1,344.5	1	1	0
1	1	0	842.8	Unionville, N.Y.	10988	0.4	1,335.0	3	2	1
3	2	1	866.4	Branchville, N.J.	07826	3.4	1,311.9	4	3	1
4	3	1	894.7	Delaware Water Gap, Pa.	18327	0.1	1,283.6	2	1	1
2	1	1	910.3	Wind Gap, Pa.	18091	1.0	1,268.0	3	2	1
3	2	1	930.8	Palmerton, Pa.	18071	2.0	1,247.5	1	0	0
1	0	0	931.1	Slatington, Pa.	18080	2.0	1,247.2	4	3	1
4	3	1	961.6	Blue Rocks Campground		1.5	1,216.7	1	0	0
1	1	0	971.1	Port Clinton, Pa.	19549		1,207.2	3	2	1
3	2	1	994.8	Pine Grove, Pa.	17963	3.7	1,183.5	6	4	2
6	4	2	1,041.0	Duncannon, Pa.	17020		1,137.3	3	2	1
3	2	1	1,066.7	Boiling Springs, Pa.	17007		1,111.6	1	1	0
1	1	0	1,075.5	Mt. Holly Springs, Pa.	17065	2.5	1,102.8	5	3	1

SOUTHBOUND Days from last point at 8	12	25 miles per day	Miles from Katahdin	DROP POINT	ZIP Code	Miles off A.T.	Miles from Springer	NORTHBOUND Days from last point at 8	12	25 miles per day
5	3	1	1,106.0	Fayetteville, Pa.	17222	3.5	1,072.3	1	1	0
1	1	0	1,110.7	South Mountain, Pa.	17261	1.2	1,067.6	2	1	1
2	1	1	1,121.3	Blue Ridge Summit, Pa.	17214	1.2	1,057.0	1	0	0
1	0	0	1,124.1	Cascade, Md.	21719	1.7	1,054.2	2	1	0
2	1	0	1,133.9	Smithsburg, Md.	21783	2.4	1,044.4	2	2	1
2	2	1	1,147.4	Boonsboro, Md.	21713	2.4	1,030.9	3	2	1
3	2	1	1,165.5	Harpers Ferry, W.Va.	25425	0.5	1,012.8	3	2	1
				ATC Headquarters		0.2				
3	2	1	1,184.6	Bluemont, Va.	20135	1.7	993.7	4	3	1
4	3	1	1,212.4	Linden, Va.	22642	1.0	965.9	1	1	0
1	1	0	1,218.8	Front Royal, Va.	22630	4.2	959.5	14	10	5
14	10	5	1,3258	Waynesboro, Va.	22980	4.5	852.5	6	4	2
6	4	2	1,364.9	Montebello, Va.	24464	2.5	813.4	4	2	1
4	2	1	1,381.2	Buena Vista, Va.	24416	9.3	797.1	5	3	2
5	3	2	1,403.0	Glasgow, Va.	24555	5.9	775.3	6	4	2
				Big Island, Va.	24526	4.7				
6	4	2	1,438.0	Buchanan, Va.	24066	5.0	740.3	3	2	1

SOUTHBOUND Days from last point at 8 12 25 miles per day			Miles from Katahdin	DROP POINT	ZIP Code	Miles off A.T.	Miles from Springer	NORTHBOUND Days from last point at 8 12 25 miles per day		
3	2	1	1,458.2	Troutville, Va.	24175	1.3	720.1	0	0	0
0	0	0	1,459.7	Cloverdale, Va.	24077	1.0	718.6	3	2	1
3	2	1	1,479.5	Catawba, Va.	24070	1.0	698.8	9	6	3
9	6	3	1,552.4	Pearisburg, Va.	24134	1.0	625.9	6	4	2
6	4	2	1,595.3	Bastian, Va.	24314	2.7	583.0	6	4	2
				Bland, Va.	24315	2.5				
6	4	2	1,640.0	Atkins, Va.	24311	3.2	538.3	2	1	1
2	1	1	1,651.5	Sugar Grove, Va.	24375	3.2	526.8	3	2	1
3	2	1	1,666.1	Troutdale, Va.	24378	2.6	512.2	6	4	2
6	4	2	1,715.3	Damascus, Va.	24236		463.0	2	2	1
2	2	1	1,730.3	Shady Valley, Tenn.	37688	2.7	448.0	4	3	1
4	3	1	1,756.8	Hampton, Tenn.	37658	2.0	421.5	1	1	0
1	1	0	1,765.7	Dennis Cove, USFS 50		0.2	412.6	3	2	1
3	2	1	1,790.1	Roan Mountain, Tenn.	37687	3.4	388.2	7	5	2
7	5	2	1,838.4	Erwin, Tenn.	37650	3.8	339.9	9	6	3
9	6	3	1,906.5	Hot Springs, N.C.	28743		271.8	4	3	1
4	3	1	1,942.3	Davenport Gap			236.0	6	4	2

SOUTHBOUND Days from last point at 8	12	25 miles per day	Miles from Katahdin	DROP POINT	ZIP Code	Miles off A.T.	Miles from Springer	NORTHBOUND Days from last point at 8	12	25 miles per day
6	4	2	1,973.6	Gatlinburg, Tenn.	37738	15.0	204.7	7	5	2
7	5	2	2,015.7	Fontana Dam, N.C.	28733	1.8	162.6	4	2	1
4	2	1	2,043.3	Nantahala Outdoor Center			135.0	5	3	1
5	3	1	2,070.6	Franklin, N.C.	28734	10.0	107.7	8	5	2
6	4	2	2,110.8	Hiawassee, Ga.	30546	11.0	67.5	5	3	1
5	3	1	2,127.4	Helen, Ga.	30545	9.0	50.9	4	2	1
4	2	1	2,147.6	Neels Gap, Walasi-Yi Center	28734		30.7	2	1	1
2	1	1	2,158.2	Suches, Ga.	30572	2.0	20.1	3	2	1
3	2	1	2,178.3	Springer Mountain Terminus			0.0			
1	0	0	2,187.1	Amicalola Falls State Park			8.8			

Prepared Foods

Many products that are convenient for hikers can be purchased off the grocery shelf and mailed with no additional preparation or purchased during your hike. In the menus in Chapter Four, many items appear that were not home-made or prepared at home. You should feel free to experiment with those and similar convenience foods as you plan menus for your own hike.

Meat and protein products

GranBurger or Nature's Burger—*Available at vegetarian markets, both of those are vegetarian hamburger alternatives or granualized protein and can be carried dry. Our hikers added water and used them as patties until the hamburger buns I sent started turning green. Later, they mixed them into grain and noodle dishes.*

Smoky Links—*Widely available by a number of brand names, our hikers used these cooked smoked sausages in meals or ate them without additional preparation.*

Top Shelf dinners—*The hikers liked this brand of canned chicken, turkey, or pork dinners.*

Salami or sausage chub—*A "chub" is another name for a roll of sausage. There are many brands.*

Beef sticks—*Many brands of this summer sausage will do. Hickory Farms is the best known.*

Mountain House beef stew—*A freeze-dried stew available at backpacking stores or from mail-order suppliers.*

Oxtail soup

Pepperoni—*available sliced, in packets, or as sticks that hikers slice as needed.*

Egg powder

Pasta, breads, vegetables and grain products

Pilot biscuits—*These hard, flat biscuits were not a particular favorite, but they come freeze-dried and last well and are available by mail order or over the Internet.*

Blueberry pancakes—*The plastic bottles made by companies such as Bisquick, to which you just add water, shake, and pour, are convenient for hikers.*

Lipton Noodles & Sauce (alfredo flavor)

Rice-a-Roni

Tuna Helper

Dried tomato flakes

Dried mushrooms

Cereals and breakfast foods

Grape Nuts

Breakfast bars—*We sent straw-berry, cherry, and other fruit flavors; many brands and varieties are available off the shelf from companies such as Carnation.*

6-layer bars

Almond bars

Apricot bars

Bran bars

Butterscotch bars

Chewy granola bars

Crunchy granola bars

Honey-nut bars

Instant apple-cinnamon oat bran

Instant grits

Instant oatmeal

Lemon bars

Snacks and Desserts

Chex Party Mix—*We used the Wheat Chex version, available prepackaged in stores.*

peanut krisps/oat krisps

Astronaut ice cream (freeze-dried)

Cheddar cheese snack crackers

Chinese cookies

Chocolate chip cookies

Coconut cream pudding

Cracker Jack

Fig bars

Fudge bars

Graham crackers (spread with peanut butter)

Jell-O

Lemon pudding

Macaroon bars

No-bake cheesecake

No-bake chocolate mint pie

No-bake chocolate mousse

Nutrilite bars (an Amway product)

Peanut brittle

Peppermint treats

Pop Tarts

Powdered syrup—*available at backpacking stores*

PowerBars

Pralines

Sour-cream packet

Sunbelt Bar

Taco shells

Tiger's Milk Bars

Toffee bars

Wheatsworth Crackers

Sources for Supplies

Prices for freeze-dried and prepackaged foods are better when you buy in bulk but tend to be expensive even so. Here are some Web sites and addresses of companies that sold backpacking foods and dried foods as of January 2009. This listing does not imply a recommendation on the part of the author or publisher. As with any mail-order or Internet purchase, shop with prudence and common sense.

Alpine Aire Foods
4041-B Alvis Court
Rocklin, CA 95677
(800) 322-6325

Backpacker's Pantry
<www.backpackerspantry.com>
6350 Gunpark Drive
Boulder, CO 80301
(303) 581-0518

The Baker's Catalogue
(source for 8 oz. dried eggs)
58 Billings Farm Road
White River Junction, VT 05001
(800) 827-6836

BackWoods Grocery
120 Interstate North Parkway SE,
Suite 304
Atlanta, GA 30339
(770) 612-8000
(888) 820-0139

Campmor
<www.campmor.com>
P.O. Box 680
Mahwah, NJ 07430
(800) 525-4784

Caribou Cry
<www.cariboucry.com>
671 10th Street
West Owen Sound, Ontario
N4K 3R8 CANADA

The Internet Grocer
<www.internet-grocer.net>
1737 Cascade Street
Mesquite, TX 75149
(903) 356-6443

LDP Camping Foods
<www.ldpcampingfoods.com>
113 Gill Dr.
Lafayette, LA 70507
(800) 826-5767

Mountain House Oregon Freeze
Dry, Inc.
P.O. Box 1048
Albany, OR 97321
(800) 547-4060

Weider Nutrition International
(Tiger's Milk Bars)
Salt Lake City, UT 84104
(800) 695-7888

A good Web site for finding organic and natural foods is <www.allorganiclinks.com>.

Bibliography

Antell, Steve. *Backpacker's Recipe Book*. Boulder: Pruett, 1980.

Axcell, C., D. Cooke, and V. Kinmont. *Simple Foods for the Pack*. San Francisco: Sierra Club Books, 1986.

Fleming, June. *The Well-Fed Backpacker*. New York: Random, 1986.

Gunn, Carolyn. *The Expedition Cookbook*. Denver: Chockstone P, 1988.

Lappe, Frances Moore. *Diet for a Small Planet*. New York: Ballantine Books, 1975.

Mettugh, Gretchen. *The Hungry Hiker's Book of Good Cooking*. New York: Alfred A. Knopf, 1982.

Prater, Y., and R. D. Mendenhall. *Gorp, Glop, and Glue Stew*. Seattle: Mountaineers, 1986.

Ross, Cindy, and Todd Gladfelter. *A Hiker's Companion*. Seattle: The Mountaineers, 1993.

Photography Credits

Index

1 **Easy Granola**

Serve cold with water and powdered milk, or add hot water for a hot breakfast, or eat dry as a snack.

2 **Spotted Applesauce**

Add water to Package 1 ingredients to cover. Bring water to boil, then simmer until tender (about 5 minutes). Top with nuts (Package 2). Can soak ingredients overnight in water to cover.

3 **Ralston Cereal**

Heat $2\frac{1}{4}$ cups water to boiling. Stir in Package 1 (Ralston and salt) and return to boil. Remove pan from heat. Cover, and let stand until cereal thickens. Add Packages 2, 3, and 4 (milk, nuts, and raisins).

4 **Scrambled Eggs**

Blend with $\frac{1}{3}$ cup water. Let set 10 minutes. Beat with fork. Cook in skillet in which 1 tablespoon margarine has been melted.

Tear along perforations, and include recipes in packages.

Campsite Cooking Instructions 1–8

5 **Sunrise Spuds**

Boil 1 cup water. Put all ingredients in bowl and pour in boiling water. Fluff with fork, and serve.

6 **Wheat Cereal**

Boil 4 cups water. Stir in package. Add 2 tablespoons margarine, return to boil. Cover pot, remove from heat, and let stand 5-10 minutes.

7 **Muesli**

Add water to package ingredients to eat as breakfast cereal, or eat as dry snack.

8 **Cream of Wheat**

Heat $2\frac{1}{4}$ cups water to boiling. Add Package 1 slowly, stirring constantly. Cook $2\frac{1}{2}$ minutes or until thickened. Stir in Package 2.

9 Instant Oatmeal

Add boiling water to the mix in cup or container. Stir and enjoy. Cooking isn't really necessary, since a few minutes in hot water softens everything nicely. Add dried fruits, if desired.

10 Arroz con Queso

Add Package 1 and 2 tablespoons margarine to 4 cups water. Bring to boil. Simmer covered 15 minutes (less if using instant rice). Serve on tortilla chips (Package 3). Sprinkle cheese (Package 2) on top.

11 Camper's Lentil Stew

Mix all ingredients with 4 cups water. Bring to boil, and simmer, covered 20 minutes.

12 Chicken and Nut Stir Pot

Add Package 1 to 3 cups water and margarine. Bring to boil. Lower heat, and cook 15 minutes or until rice is tender, stirring frequently. Add nuts as desired.

Tear along perforations, and include recipes in packages..

Campsite Cooking Instructions 9–16

13 Chicken and Rice Curry

Combine all with 1 tablespoon margarine and $3\frac{1}{4}$ cups water, and bring to boil. Simmer 15 minutes (covered), stirring occasionally.

14 Chicken Klister with Peas

Bring $3\frac{1}{2}$ cups water and Package 1 to boil. Simmer 15 minutes. Meanwhile, add $\frac{1}{2}$ cup cold water to sour cream, and beat with fork for 1 minute. Stir in almonds and sour cream just before serving.

15 Chicken Rag-Out

Simmer all ingredients in 3 cups water for 15 minutes. Add more water if necessary.

16 Chicken Stew

Bring Package 1 and $1\frac{1}{2}$ tablespoon margarine boil in $3\frac{1}{2}$ cups water. Simmer 15 minutes. Stir in Package 2 until just moistened. Let rest 1 minute, and fluff with fork.

17 Chili-to-Go

Add 2 cups water to the 2 cups dried chili. Stir and bring to boil. Cover and cook slowly 10 minutes. Prepare Lipton Noodles & Sauce (Package 2) according to packet directions.

18 Chipped Beef and Broccoli Dish

Boil 3 cups water and 2 tablespoons margarine. Add Package 1, and cook 10 minutes, stirring as needed. Chop $1/2$ packet chipped beef (Package 2), and add to Package 1 the last couple minutes of cooking time. (Save the other half for use another day.) Add more water if needed.

19 Chipped Beef and Creamed Peas

In one pot, chop beef (Package 1) and add Package 2 (peas) and $2 1/2$ cups water. Bring to boil. Simmer 15 minutes. In small pot, stir together Package 3 (white sauce) and $1 1/2$ cup water. Boil, then simmer 1 minute, stirring constantly. Stir in Package 4 (potatoes) and white sauce.

20 Chipped Beef Stew

Cook Package 1 (soup and vegetables) in 3 to $3 1/2$ cups water 15 minutes. Chop chipped beef (Package 2). Add extra $1/2$ cup water and chipped beef to the cooked soup mixture.

Tear along perforations, and include recipes in packages.

Campsite Cooking Instructions 17–24

21 Corn Chowder

Add Package 1 (vegetables) to 4 cups water. Bring to boil, and simmer 15 minutes. Add Package 2 (milk and potatoes), and simmer a few more minutes. Add 2 tablespoons margarine.

22 Curried Vegetables

Mix Package 1 (soup) with $2 1/4$ cups water. Bring to a boil, stirring occasionally. Simmer 10 minutes. Remove from heat, and stir in Package 2 (rice). Let stand 5 minutes. Add raisins and nuts, sprinkle coconut on top.

23 Deb's African Peanut Stew

Bring 3 cups water and Package 1 (chicken) to boil, and simmer 15 minutes. Stir in Package 2 (peanut butter).

24 Expedition Spaghetti

Bring $3 1/2$ cups water and Packages 1 and 2 (spaghetti and sauce) to boil. Cook ten minutes. Remove from heat. Stir in Package 3 (soup). Sprinkle cheese over all.

25 Fontana Dinner

Bring 3 cups water and Package 1 (rice and vegetables) to boil, and simmer until tender, 12-15 minutes. Top with Package 2 (shredded cheese). Serve when cheese has melted.

26 Green Pea-Brown Rice Mix

Add 2 cups water and margarine to Package 1 (rice). Bring to boil. Lower heat and simmer 20 minutes. Serve with nuts (Package 2).

27 Hashed Brown Potatoes

In pan, cover Package 1 with boiling water. Let stand for 20 minutes. Drain. Stir in Package 2. In skillet, heat margarine. Spread potato mix evenly in hot skillet. Stir slowly until underside is golden brown. Turn, and brown other side.

28 Hawaiian Chicken

Bring 2 cups water, 1 tablespoon margarine, and Package 1 (chicken) to boil. Simmer 10 minutes. Stir in Package 2 (rice), and remove from heat. Add more water if necessary. Let stand 5 minutes. Add cashews (Package 3).

Campsite Cooking Instructions 25–32

Tear along perforations, and include recipes in packages.

29 Isle Royale Dinner

In 3$\frac{1}{2}$ cups water, add package, bring to boil, and simmer 15 minutes.

30 Kasha

Add ingredients to 1$\frac{1}{4}$ cup of water and 1 tablespoon of margarine. Bring to boil and simmer, covered, 15 minutes, stirring occasionally.

31 Manhattan Clam Chowder

Cook Package 1 in 3 cups water for 10 minutes. Add Package 2 and undrained clams (Package 3). Cook 5 additional minutes. Add more water if needed.

32 Mountain Chowder

Add Package 1 (vegetables) to 3 cups of water. Bring water to a boil, and simmer 15 minutes. Add Package 2 (potatoes), and simmer a few more minutes.

33 Safari Surprise

Mix Packages 1, 2, and 3 in 3 cups water. Bring to boil, and simmer 15 minutes. Stir in Package 4, and let stand 5 minutes.

34 Shrimp Rice Dinner

Bring 2 cups of water to a boil. Stir in Package 1 (rice). (If using dried shrimp, add now.) Cover, and let sit for 10 min-utes. Drain canned shrimp (Package 2). Add to rice mix-ture. Stir, and cover for 5 minutes. Add margarine if desired.

35 Spanish Rice

Bring 3¼ cups and all ingredients to boil in pot, and simmer 15 minutes.

36 St. Patrick's Stew

Boil 4 cups water and Package 1 (noodles); cook 8 minutes. Add more water if needed. Stir in almonds and raisins, and serve.

Campsite Cooking Instructions 33–40

Tear along perforations, and include recipes in packages.

37 Stroganoff

Mix 1½ cups water to Package 1 (stroganoff mix) in small pot. Heat, and simmer until sauce thickens. Cover, and remove from heat. Add Package 2 (beef and noodles) to 3 cups water in large pot. Bring to boil, and simmer 15 minutes. Stir in sauce. Add margarine.

38 Turkey Trail Dinner

Combine Package 1 (chicken) with 3 cups water and 2 tablespoons margarine. Bring to boil, and simmer 10 minutes. Remove from heat. Stir in Package 2 (stuffing). Cover, and let stand 5 minutes.

39 Tuna Fettuccini

Bring 3 cups water and Package 1 to boil, and simmer 12 minutes. Add 1 cup water to Package 2 in small pan. Stirring constantly, bring to boil, and simmer on low heat 1 minute. Stir into tuna mixture, and serve.

40 White Mountain Stew

Bring 3½ cups water and Package 1 (vegetables) to boil, and simmer 15 minutes. Add couscous (Package 2) and simmer 5 additional minutes. Serve with generous helping of margarine and salt.